Writing History

Fifth Edition

Writing History

A Guide for
Canadian Students

William Kelleher Storey • Mairi Cowan

OXFORD
UNIVERSITY PRESS

Oxford University Press is a department of the University of Oxford.
It furthers the University's objective of excellence in research, scholarship,
and education by publishing worldwide. Oxford is a registered trade mark of
Oxford University Press in the UK and in certain other countries.

Published in Canada by
Oxford University Press
8 Sampson Mews, Suite 204,
Don Mills, Ontario M3C 0H5 Canada

www.oupcanada.com

Copyright © Oxford University Press Canada 2019

The moral rights of the authors have been asserted

Database right Oxford University Press (maker)

Adapted from a work originally published by Oxford University Press, Ltd.
This adapted version has been customized for Canada only and is published by
arrangement with Oxford University Press Ltd. It may not be sold elsewhere.
Copyright © 1996 by the President and Fellows of Harvard University.
Copyright © 2016, 2013, 2009, 2005, 1999 by Oxford University Press, Inc.

First Edition published in 2004
Second Edition published in 2008
Third Edition published in 2011
Fourth Edition published in 2016

Library and Archives Canada Cataloguing in Publication

Title: Writing history : a guide for Canadian students / William Kelleher Storey and Mairi Cowan.
Names: Storey, William Kelleher, author. | Cowan, Mairi, 1974- editor.
Description: Fifth edition. | Includes bibliographical references and index.
Identifiers: Canadiana (print) 20189066776 | Canadiana (ebook) 20190063602 |
ISBN 9780199033737 (softcover) | ISBN 9780199033744 (EPUB)
Subjects: LCSH: History—Research. | LCSH: History—Research—Canada. |
LCSH: Academic writing. | LCSH: Historiography.
Classification: LCC D16 S76 2019 | DDC 907.2—dc23

Cover and interior design: Sherill Chapman

Oxford University Press is committed to our environment.
This book is printed on Forest Stewardship Council® certified paper
and comes from responsible sources.

Printed and bound in the United States of America

1 2 3 4 — 22 21 20 19

Contents

Preface to the Fifth Canadian Edition

As the conventions of writing history change, so too must the advice we give to those who are learning the craft. In this new edition of *Writing History: A Guide for Canadian Students*, we have taken the basic structure of the US edition, adapted it with material drawn from the most recent Canadian edition, and introduced additional features to ensure that the advice being presented remains consistent with current best practices.

Several significant modifications in this fifth Canadian edition help bring *Writing History* up to date with the expectations of history instructors and the needs of their students. One important change is in the selection of examples that illustrate authentic historical problems and good historical writing. To make this book more relevant not only to students of Canadian history, but also to students studying histories of other places, we now supply a better balance of Canadian and non-Canadian examples and a wider representation of different periods, places, and approaches. Other changes extend the book's usefulness for today's students with practical advice on how to face challenges both in print and online. We propose realistic guidelines to help students find, select, and use sources from academic libraries and the Internet at large, and we offer suggestions for editing that take into account both the page and the screen. Three appendices provide further guidance in conveniently condensed form. The first appendix helps students better understand the different kinds of history assignments typically given in university and college courses. The second is a citation guide that combines basic instruction on when and how to write notes and bibliographies with samples of citations formatted in accordance with the latest edition of *The Chicago Manual of Style*. The third appendix is a list of suggested resources for research and writing that students can use as starting points in their projects. We have adjusted language throughout the book to reflect contemporary usage, while acknowledging that tensions sometimes arise when new ideas begin to challenge old presumptions in the politically charged world of historical writing.

Much of the material in this edition comes directly from the work of William Kelleher Storey and Towser Jones in earlier editions: it is their wisdom and care that have made *Writing History* so helpful to so many students since its first publication in 1999. For the adaptations and additions that I have been able to supply, I owe a debt of gratitude to many people. The historians I've had the privilege to learn from and the students I've had the honour to teach have provided more insight than I can measure. Some of the best observations about what real students find genuinely helpful have come from teaching assistants, and I hope that they will find here a serviceable guide for when they are teaching the skills of research and writing. I would like to thank the people at Oxford University Press for giving me the opportunity to work on this book, and particularly Peter Chambers and Elizabeth Ferguson, who have been kindly and calmly supportive throughout the process. I would also like to extend my thanks to my colleagues at the University of Toronto, especially those in the department of Historical Studies at the University of Toronto Mississauga, for allowing me to teach history in an environment made rich by both tradition and innovation. And finally, as always, I thank my friends and family for being always there.

Mairi Cowan
University of Toronto Mississauga

Introduction

What is history? No single definition is universally accepted, but historians do generally agree on several points. History is not a compilation of names and dates to be memorized and regurgitated. Nor is it the simple description of "what happened" in the past. History is more than a matter of opinion or a declaration of right and wrong answers. It demands critical analysis, questioning and exploration, selection, debate, and interpretation. It reflects the time in which it is written, but remains true to the time it interprets.

Historians study the human past, ancient and recent, to understand not only what happened, but how and why, what it means and why it matters. And it does matter. Understanding the past gives us a basis for understanding the present. In the words of Canadian historian Margaret MacMillan, "history is not a dead subject. . . . [It] lies under the present, silently shaping our institutions, our ways of thought, our likes and dislikes."[1]

The craft of history requires making decisions. First, historians choose the subjects they think are most important. Then they select the source materials they judge most likely to shed useful light on those subjects. After carefully analyzing all the evidence they can find, they develop arguments and draw conclusions in the light of that evidence. Finally, they decide how they will present their arguments in a way that balances respect for their subjects with the needs of their readers.

The best historians are so skilled at making choices that they can transform painstaking research into seamless arguments and narratives. But don't be fooled: the decisions that fill the process of writing are difficult, and writing history well takes a lot of time and patience.

The art of selection has been central to Western historical writing ever since the time of the ancient Greeks. When the Athenian general Thucydides composed his history of the

Peloponnesian Wars, around 400 BCE, he could hardly report everything that had taken place over thirty years of battles and defeats. Instead, he chose to focus on decisive moments. Among these was the famous eulogy for the Athenian dead delivered by the statesman and general Pericles:

> I have no wish to make a long speech on subjects familiar to you all: so I shall say nothing about the warlike deeds by which we acquired our power or the battles in which we or our fathers gallantly resisted our enemies, Greek or foreign. What I want to do is, in the first place, to discuss the spirit in which we faced our trials and also our constitution and the way of life which has made us great. After that I shall speak in praise of the dead.[2]

Thucydides chose to make this speech a part of his history not just because it was moving, but because he believed it to be instructive on the nature of Athenian democracy.

Like Thucydides, historians also choose subjects that they believe can shed light on the causes of change over time. To that end, they must learn how to find sources, how to report on them faithfully, and how to use them to make inferences about the past. Their approaches vary widely, and can incorporate methods and insights not only from other historians but from scholars in the humanities, the social sciences, and the natural sciences as well. Even historians who all work in the same narrow geographical and chronological specialties approach their subjects from many different perspectives. In fact, the variety of angles from which historians approach their subjects is almost endless, and therefore, not surprisingly, historians frequently disagree with one another. Such debates are so common that there is a whole subfield of the discipline called **historiography**, the study of writing history—in a sense, the history of history. Despite the diversity of their approaches, however, all historians share a commitment to accurate reporting, persuasive argument, and clear communication. In short, all historians share a commitment to good research and writing.

Writing History is designed to introduce students to the discipline of history and its challenges. Chapter by chapter, the book explains the processes of planning; finding a topic; researching, analyzing, and incorporating sources; building arguments; and creating a finished work. Appendices offer additional help with an explanation of conventions in typical kinds of history assignments, a citation guide, and suggested further resources for research and writing. Key terms are bolded at first use and clearly defined in a glossary at the end of the book, while boxes at the end of each chapter highlight its key points.

There may be times in your studies when you find it useful to read this book straight through, and other times when you turn to it instead for answers to specific questions. However you use *Writing History*, we hope that it serves you as a helpful guide to learning and writing about the human past.

Notes

1. Margaret MacMillan, *The Uses and Abuses of History* (Toronto: Viking Canada, 2008), xi.
2. Thucydides, *The Peloponnesian War*, trans. Rex Warner (New York: Penguin Books, 1954; repr. 1984), 145.

1

Getting Started

There are many reasons to write history. Historians may be interested in explaining a particular source, in which case they must assess its significance in light of other sources. Perhaps they begin with an analytical problem that they have noticed in some body of historical literature, or with a contemporary problem affecting the world in which they live, and then they must seek out sources as a way of exploring the problem. In any case, the only way to write history is to engage with source materials and other writers. This is challenging because it is not always a simple matter to find suitable sources and engage with the right writers. A full, careful review of the largest possible number of sources and writers will help historians express ideas confidently, and this chapter provides guidance for how to start that review and choose a topic for a research essay. (There are several types of assignments that history instructors commonly set. Students who are working on primary source analyses, book or article reviews, annotated bibliographies, historiographical papers, reading response journals, research proposals, oral presentations, posters, or final exams can refer to Appendix A, "Different Kinds of History Assignments.")

Sometimes a research essay is limited to the scope of the course. At other times, such as with an honours thesis, the subject of the paper can be more open-ended. The details of an assignment may vary, which means that students will need to pay careful attention to their instructor's prompts, but they should remember that writing about history is about providing analysis, not just collecting facts.

Explore Your Interests

People are probably asking you about your interests all the time. At a party, you might find that the best approach is to condense your interests into a crisp one-liner. When you write history, you will grapple with topics and questions that cannot be summarized so neatly. Research projects present opportunities to clarify and deepen your interests.

Historians become interested in research topics for all sorts of reasons. The history of medicine may interest you because you want to become a doctor; the history of physics may interest you because you are concerned about nuclear proliferation. Perhaps some historians have inspired your interests, through either their teaching or their writing. Or an instructor may simply be requiring you to write about a specific topic. Whatever the motivation, use your sources to address questions that are significant to you and relevant to the task at hand.

Move from a Historical Interest to a Research Topic

There is so much history to write about, and so little time for writing. If you are going to get your assignment done in a reasonable time and space (ideally by the due date and within the page limit), you need to convert your historical interests into a feasible research topic. Focus your research early. Find a small story within your broad range of interests, and select only the best sources to support your interpretation.

Imagine that your instructor has asked you to write a research essay. You can either start with a broad scope and then narrow your focus until you have a topic that is the right size for the assignment, or you can start with one specific question or a single source and then expand your focus until you have enough material to complete your investigation.

If you decide to begin with a broad scope, you will need to survey the state of the field. The Internet makes possible a quick search on a search engine like Google, followed by a link to Wikipedia. This may seem like a good beginning to many people, but to historians this is merely a preliminary glance at what lies on the surface. Good writing starts with extensive and methodical reading: the more books, articles, and **primary sources** we read, the more authoritatively we may write. And good writing requires active reading, which involves taking notes, tracking down references, and observing contradictions between authors. These contradictions are especially important. Two historians writing about the same topic rarely come to the same interpretation. Why are their views conflicting? An investigation of this question can lead you to a better understanding of what we know about the past, and to a research topic that will work for your assignment. Did the historians consider different evidence? Do they have opposing political commitments? Is there a way for you to test their arguments on another set of data and come to a conclusion of your own? Maybe all historians writing about a topic agree about some things, but your personal knowledge of the subject causes you to doubt their findings. Can you support your conflicting view with evidence?

If you already have a specific question or single source in mind, you can begin from here, but you will still need sources to provide background and support. What evidence must be considered when answering your question? What context is necessary to understand the source? Are there any theoretical approaches that will shed light on your investigation?

Whether you choose to work inward from a breadth of possibilities, or outward from a precise problem, the early stages of your research process will involve the selection of reliable sources.

Work with Bibliographies

Many students begin their research by searching the Internet, yet there is so much out there, and it can be difficult to determine which sources are reliable. It is often better to start with bibliographies, lists of readings that scholars assemble for fellow researchers.

Let us say that you have been fascinated by bison ever since a childhood visit to Wood Buffalo National Park. Let us also say that, like many citizens, you are concerned about cross-cultural relations and the environment. You have read Alfred W. Crosby's *The Columbian Exchange and* Theodore Binnema's *Common and Contested Ground: A Human and Environmental History of the Northwestern Plains*,[1] and you now share their interest in relations between settlers and Indigenous peoples. You recognize that it took these historians many years of research and hundreds of pages of writing to cover their topics, and therefore you know that you will need to find something smaller in scale for your project. Neither book has much to say about bison or people in Western Canada. Their bibliographies contain some sources that will be useful for context or comparison, but they focus on different regions from your topic and, even in the most recent editions, do not include anything written more recently than the early 2000s. How can you find a **bibliography** that will lead you to current scholarship on the environmental history of the plains in Western Canada?

Ask a librarian. Librarians will probably not have a lot of narrowly specialized knowledge on your topic, but they will know how to find a good bibliography. A keyword search that combines "environmental history" with the words "bibliography," "companion," and "handbook" returns a number of promising sources, among them a book called *The Oxford Handbook of Environmental History*.[2] Go find the book in the library or online. It turns out to be rather thick, but a quick glance at the table of contents points to one chapter, called "Seas of Grass: Grasslands in World Environmental History," written by Andrew Isenberg, that looks especially promising. When you read it, you find that the essay compares the environmental history of grasslands in different parts of the world, including the Eurasian Steppes, the Pampas of South America, and the North American Great Plains. Its bibliography will lead you to additional sources.

It would be perfectly appropriate for you to start tracking down those sources and skimming them in order to narrow your topic even further. It may also be more practical—and more enjoyable—simply to ask your professor for suggestions. Chances are your professor will be happy to discuss a research topic, especially if you have a working bibliography and are developing specific ideas about your interests. Professors will be familiar with key works by other scholars and will be able to suggest books that provide helpful overviews and contain useful bibliographies. In the case of the environmental history of the plains in Canada, the first book many professors will recommend is James Daschuk's *Clearing the Plains: Disease, Politics of Starvation, and the Loss of Aboriginal Life*.[3]

As you begin to read Daschuk's book, you notice that it is comprehensive and accessible, much like Crosby's and Binnema's books, and also that it interweaves environmental history with political and social history. A careful review of the text and references even reveals that Daschuk cites both Crosby's and Binnema's books as important predecessors. Read Daschuk's book with an eye to narrowing your topic. What specific issues capture your attention? What passages do you find inspiring? In his chapter "Canada, the Northwest, and the Treaty Period, 1869–76," Daschuk writes about positions taken by the Cree in negotiating Treaty 6. Your interest is piqued by his assertion that "to the bulk of the Cree leadership, the successful negotiation of a treaty represented their best hope for survival in the new economic order on the plains." In the paragraph immediately preceding this statement, you find evidence that Cree leaders were well aware of profound economic changes sweeping over the plains and their need to respond:

> The possibility of bloodshed was real, but most of the Cree who attended the treaty talks recognized the futility of armed resistance to dominion authority. Mistawassis stressed this point to Poundmaker and The Badger, two opponents of the treaty: "We are few in numbers compared to former times, by wars and the terrible ravages of smallpox. . . . Even if it were possible to gather all the tribes together, to throw away the hand that is offered to help us, we would be too weak to make

our demands heard." Chief Ahtahkakoop echoed the sentiments of Mistawassis: "We are weak and my brother Mista-wa-sis I think is right that the buffalo will be gone before many snows. What then will be left us with which to bargain?"[4]

In this section, Daschuk cites several modern works about the Treaty 6 negotiations as well as an original source from the nineteenth century, Peter Erasmus's *Buffalo Days and Nights*. Erasmus worked as a translator for the Plains Cree during the Treaty 6 negotiations, so his book seems promising, given your interests. The next step is to search for Erasmus's book, as well as other books, by following the clues in Daschuk's bibliography and **footnotes** and then looking up these works in the library's online **catalogue.**

Spend Time in an Academic Library

Perhaps the best place to find additional sources is in your own academic institution's library, where you will find a wealth of materials. Since an academic library is designed for student and faculty research, the resources that are available to you will almost certainly be more extensive than those in a public library. You are likely to find many excellent sources including both general and specialized reference works online and perhaps in hard copy, books on the shelves (usually called "the stacks"), e-books, journal articles, films, and so on.

Speak with a Librarian

Since library holdings change constantly, it's a good idea to talk with a librarian—a research specialist—before you begin to search the catalogue. Librarians are the unsung heroes of the historical world and historians depend heavily on them, because they not only preserve information but also know how it is organized and how to access it. They can be an enormous help to historians and students in finding what they need. This is particularly important to emphasize in today's world, when electronic information is increasing exponentially and ways to access it are changing constantly. Reference librarians are experts in electronic searches, and most will be happy to show you how to begin. You will save yourself a lot of time and maximize the likelihood of finding good sources by consulting a librarian at the outset of your project.

Explore the Library Catalogue

The key to searching a catalogue is understanding how the information is organized. Not all libraries arrange their materials the same way, but most items in the library are listed by author, title, and subject heading.

1. **Find Books by Subject Heading.** To find the right headings, start with a keyword search. In a keyword search, it is important to use distinctive words. Type in *environmental history* and you will get too many entries. A more specific search, like *Canadian environmental history*, will still produce too many. But if you find one book from among the many entries that fits with your topic and click the subject headings associated with that entry, you will be taken to other works on the same subject. Note that subject searches differ from keyword searches. Keyword searches may turn up your word or words in widely varying order. By contrast, subject headings are fixed by the Library of Congress, and you will get a hit on a subject heading only if you click on or type in its exact wording. (All librarians will be able to explain to you how to search for Library of Congress subject headings.) For example, the subject headings for Peter Erasmus reveal a number of useful possibilities, including "Indians of North America—Canada, Western—History." A click on that link offers more books about the subject. These books, in turn, can be looked up simply by clicking them. If your own library does not own the book, ask a librarian about how to order the item through Interlibrary Loan.

2. **Search Journals in Online Databases.** Articles and reviews from scholarly journals can often provide helpful guideposts to

a field. Many libraries now subscribe to **databases** that allow users to search online indexes, such as Academic Search Premier offered by EBSCOhost, JSTOR, and Project MUSE. Sometimes these services grant users access to full-text versions of articles. When articles are not available through the databases, the system provides citations that allow users to find hard-copy versions of the articles or to order them through interlibrary loan. Full-text versions of journal articles are available through many databases, which together provide subscribing libraries with access to recent issues and back issues of hundreds of journals.

3.   Explore Other Online Resources. Colleges and universities buy access to controlled websites, library portals, and databases so that you can use them for research. Some of the most commonly used are listed in Appendix C, "Suggested Resources for Research and Writing in History."

One particularly useful site, available by personal or institutional subscription, is Oxford Bibliographies Online (http://www.oxfordbibliographies.com). Search this site within categories such as African American Studies, African Studies, Childhood Studies, Chinese Studies, Classics, Islamic Studies, Jewish Studies, Latin American Studies, Medieval Studies, Military History, and Renaissance and Reformation. There is no separate category for Canadian history, but depending on your topic you can find many references to Canadian history within the other categories.

For a project on cross-cultural relations and colonial North American environmental history, for example, click the box labelled "Atlantic History." (Atlantic History usually refers to the history of African, American, and European interactions from the late fifteenth century, when Columbus sailed from Spain to the Caribbean, to the late nineteenth century, when slavery ended in the Americas. As you will see from this subject area in the Oxford Bibliographies, it can extend quite far beyond the Atlantic coasts.)

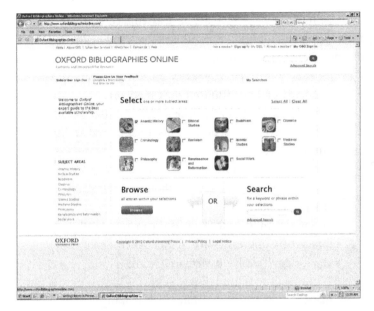

Figure 1.1

Clicking "Atlantic History" opens a table of contents. Each title represents a specialized area of Atlantic History.

Browse down and click "Environment and the Natural World." This opens a short essay by an expert scholar, Susan Scott Parrish, about Atlantic environmental history. Her essay will guide you through the next stages of research. For ease of reference, on the left a table of contents allows readers to navigate back and forth through different sections. The essay itself also contains links to sources and related essays. Other essays in the "Atlantic History" series that might prove useful to your project include "Native American Histories in North America," "Continental America," and "Hinterlands of the Atlantic World."

4. Search Historical Websites. Today there are thousands of excellent Internet sites for scholars interested in history. Archives have placed documents and images online, as have newspapers and institutions. Many scholars have assembled websites that are informative and interactive. For this project, you might find these examples particularly useful:

- Canadiana Online, http://online.canadiana.ca, provides searchable databases with access to digitized collections of books, newspapers, periodicals, images, and **archival materials**.
- http://www.virtualmuseum.ca, Canada's Virtual Museum site, provides links to several thousand museums and heritage organizations.
- One of the most extensive lists can be found at the Library of Congress "Virtual Reference Shelf," http://www.loc.gov/rr/askalib/virtualref.html.

Sites like these—and many more—are making it possible for scholars to study subjects that once required expensive research trips to distant locations.

Use Reference Sources for Background Information

Fundamental reference works, including encyclopedias, dictionaries, and textbooks, survey a broad range of interests and topics.

1.   **Encyclopedias.** A good encyclopedia can help you get an early, broad understanding of a topic. It will contain basic explanations as well as hints about related subjects. Just keep in mind that encyclopedias can provide only an introduction: a paper that relies heavily on encyclopedia articles will not impress your readers.

If you decide to use encyclopedias, consult those that are written and edited by specialists in the field and aimed at an academic readership. The *Encyclopedia of Africa*, edited by Kwame Anthony Appiah and Henry Louis Gates, Jr., and published by

Oxford University Press, for example, would be a reliable place to find some basic information on an African history topic, while the *Grove Encyclopedia of Islamic Art and Architecture* is an authoritative reference work for the field of Islamic art.

2. Dictionaries. Dictionaries are also a quick way to explore some topics. Be aware that there are different types of dictionary, each with its own special uses. *Prescriptive* dictionaries like *Webster's* tell you how words should be used; *descriptive* dictionaries like *American Heritage* tell you how words are actually used; and *historical* dictionaries like the *Oxford English Dictionary* (the OED) tell you how words have been used over time. The OED can be a valuable resource if you are reading primary sources in English and basing your argument or interpretation on specific words or phrases. Consider, for example, that "meat" once meant any solid food, "nice" was used to describe a foolish person, and an "apology" was a defence or vindication against accusation or aspersion.

Other specialized dictionaries commonly held in library reference collections may prove useful too. Some, such as *A Dictionary of Environmental History* and the *Princeton Dictionary of Ancient Egypt* would be good dictionaries to help you understand those fields better. Biographical dictionaries can help you better understand the lives of individual people. The *Dictionary of Canadian Biography* provides information about significant figures from Canada's past, and the *Dictionary of National Biography* provides information about people who lived in the British Isles.

3. Textbooks. Increasingly, history textbooks are available online, although a traditional bound version will do nicely in this case. Textbooks often contain useful surveys of a topic, and they also offer bibliographies. They are usually not very focused, however, nor are they generally peer-reviewed. Rather than relying on them directly, check their bibliographies for further references.

Conduct a General Search on the Internet

Most scholars with access to a computer will supplement a research project by using a high-quality search engine such as Google (http://www.google.com). Enter your keywords in the search box and Google "looks" for them on the Internet. Google then takes cached copies or "snapshots" of each relevant page and reports them back to you, in order of their relevance. Note that Google determines relevance by weighing factors that may not be relevant to historical research, such as the number of links to a site, and that Google search results now vary from person to person, depending on one's previous searches.

Search by choosing distinctive keywords. In some cases, you might want to cast a wide net and search for a general term. In other cases, you might want to search for specific names and titles. If you were writing an essay on the military history of medieval Europe, for example, you might enter the phrase "Knights Templar" in the search box. Google unearths quite a few websites that appear to be helpful, but you should proceed with caution before deciding to use them in your research.

Scan the Search Results

How do scholars know which websites are most promising? The hits may be evaluated by asking what sort of institution publishes the website. The author should represent a reputable institution that is interested in the dissemination of objective information. The institution's administration should support the Internet site and oversee its content. If that is not the case, and the website is published to entertain, make money, or spread disinformation, it must be approached more warily. One quick way to learn about an institution publishing a website is to examine the domain name, particularly the abbreviation that occurs after the institution's name. In the United States, websites that contain .edu, .ac, and .gov were created by people affiliated with academic and government institutions. These sites may or may not represent the institution's official positions, but, at the very least, the authors of the sites had to be accepted or hired by the institution. It should be noted that it is very easy to obtain a domain name ending in .org, .net, .com, and .co; anybody with a credit card may do so. These websites tend to be either commercial or personal, which means history students must treat them with great skepticism.

Get a Quick First Impression

The first click on a Google search result will reveal much about the reliability of the site. Here are some criteria to help you arrive at a quick critical assessment of sites in our search for Knights Templar on Google.

1.   **Who Is the Author?** The more you know about the author, the more likely it is that he or she is willing to stake a reputation on the contents. When an author is identified, do a follow-up search on the name in order to verify credentials and affiliations. Is the author a recognized authority on the subject of the Internet site? If not, you should not give the content much weight.

2.   **Has the Website Also Been Published in Print?** Many sites began as print sources or are published in both print and electronic editions. In these cases the quality is likely to be higher because printed information tends to have higher costs and therefore higher quality controls. Typically, it takes a great deal of time and effort to publish a printed book or journal article. Academic works of history that are published in these ways usually must meet with the approval of editors and **peer reviewers** before they are printed and distributed. For this reason, many students have gotten into the habit of trusting printed sources. By contrast, publishing on the Internet can be done cheaply and quickly, often with no controls for quality. There are virtually no barriers to publishing one's own website.

3.   **What Is the Tone of the Website?** To some degree, objectivity may be determined by the website's tone. Many websites are

written to entertain viewers or to advocate a particular point of view. Other websites are more objective but written with a different audience in mind, say, readers who are young, or who are aficionados and hobbyists. Assessing the tone of a website can be an important component of a preliminary evaluation.

4.   Does the Website Feature References? In historical scholarship, it is important for others to be able to follow in an author's footsteps. This allows us to confirm or contradict an author's findings. If there are no references, it is difficult to verify the information. It may not be reliable and therefore should not be used in a historical essay.

Critically Assess Sources on the Internet

Let us now assess some of the websites that our Google search uncovered for the Knights Templar. Some of these sources are promising, but others are not.

1.   "Knights Templar," from Wikipedia, the Free Encyclopedia. Wikipedia is now being used as a first point of reference by many history students because the first page of Google search results often references Wikipedia articles. Wikipedia is an Internet encyclopedia whose articles are written by thousands of volunteer contributors. Contributors may help to revise, update, and edit articles to ensure quality, but there is no board of editors to verify accuracy. Because Wikipedia contains mistakes that may or may not be quickly fixed, some history instructors prohibit their students from citing it as a source in their assignments. Other instructors have taken an opposite approach, encouraging their students to contribute to Wikipedia so that they will make it better. Still, it is best not to cite Wikipedia in a formal writing assignment unless you are explicitly told that you may. Reading a Wikipedia article, like reading a traditional encyclopedia article, affords a superficial orientation to a subject. Good research requires more of the researcher. In the case of the Wikipedia article about the Knights Templar, it contains descriptions of basic aspects of the medieval order and its legacy, including appearances in modern popular culture, plus links to further electronic resources. This information may help you direct your research, but if you verify each source in the "references" section independently, you will note that only some are scholarly. Overall, this Wikipedia page can serve to provide some basic background information, and it can lead you to some interesting possible research directions, but it should not be used directly without first being checked against reliable, scholarly sources.

2. Knights Templar – Facts & Summary – HISTORY.com. This is a page from the website of the History television network. It provides slick trailers from their television series on the Templars and a short description of the group's history. It is a commercial site, complete with advertisements for the television series and other products, and not signed by an author. Its named sources are newspapers, magazines, and other commercial websites—not research by scholars. The information on this site may be entertaining, but it is not appropriate for research at the university level.

3. "10 Incredible Things You Should Know About the Templars" from Realm of History. One of the first things you should notice about this site is all the ads that pop up. Right away, this should lead you to suspect that the main purpose of the site is not to educate, but to entertain and possibly generate income for the site's owner. There is an author listed, or at least a name provided after the phrase "posted by," but if you do a quick search on the Internet for this person, you will see that he is the founder of the site and describes himself as an "amateur historian." No sources are provided. This is not a good site for university-level historical research. You should ignore it and move on to more academic sources.

4. "The Knights Templar Burned in the Presence of Philip the Fair and His Courtiers." A general search on Google will turn up images related to the group. For a search dedicated completely to imagery, click on "Images" in the top left corner of the Google screen. You will be provided with many images of the Knights Templar, medieval as well as modern. The former may be worth analyzing for the purposes of the research paper. Browse the images, but take the same critical approach as with anything else on the Internet. Rely on reputable websites affiliated with recognizable, professional institutions, such as universities, libraries, museums, and art galleries. This particular link turns out to be a page from the J. Paul Getty Museum, a respected art museum in California. It presents an image from an early-fifteenth-century manuscript, and informs its readers that the image is downloadable, but it does not offer much description of the subject. You may choose to use this image as a primary source for your research, and you may also want to search for good secondary sources to help you interpret it responsibly.

Approach Your Topic from a Particular Angle

A library at a large university will contain thousands of items that pertain to many topics, and it may also have special collections of manuscripts and artifacts. Even a small library will have several dozen items for some research topics. Don't be discouraged; you simply need to bring more focus to your topic.

Think back to the books you have read and the courses you have taken. If you like to read biographies, then you might want to identify individuals who made a significant contribution to the field. If you like to read social history, you might wish to explore a topic along the lines of class, gender, or race. You might be partial to the history of a particular place or time period. Keep working in the library and on the Internet until it seems you have a manageable number of resources with which to write an essay on a reasonably focused topic.

Browse for More Sources

There is only one way to make an informed choice about a topic: go back to the Internet and to the library stacks, and browse through the potential source materials. Look for both quantity and quality. Are there enough sources to write this paper, or are there so many sources that the topic must be narrowed further? It is also important to consider when your sources were published. Are you finding the most recent scholarship, or do your sources seem old enough to be out of date?

It is probably a good idea to start with a narrow base of sources and build it into a broader base. As you search for sources in the library stacks, you will find more clues that will lead you to further sources. Just keep in mind that there are limits to your time, and there are limits to your paper. In the early stages of research, you do not need to find everything.

Form a Hypothesis

An essay based on historical research should reach new conclusions about a topic. This is a challenging proposition, and by now you may be wondering if it is worth writing a paper about your first topic of the environmental history of the Canadian plains at all. Daschuk and his fellow scholars have already written plenty about the subject. Can you bring a unique perspective to bear on the topic?

While you are identifying a topic, you should begin forming a **hypothesis**, one of the most important steps in writing a research paper. A hypothesis is not an ordinary guess; it is the proposition that can guide you through the research. As you read your sources you will have questions about your topic, and as you get answers you will refine your hypothesis. Over the course of your research, you will find that you are getting closer to forming an **argument**.

How does one arrive at a hypothesis? Start to jot down some questions. In the case of your research focusing on the negotiations for Treaty 6, you may be wondering about several things: (1) What sort of person was Peter Erasmus? (2) What was stipulated in Treaty 6? (3) Were the Treaty 6 negotiations fair or unfair? (4) What was the most significant point of disagreement in the Treaty 6 negotiations?

Now ask yourself two more things: Can you build an argument around the potential answer to one of the questions, and does the question address some broader issue in history? Questions 1 and 2 might yield only descriptions and not arguments. Question 3 could produce a debate (yes, they were fair; no, they were unfair), but such a debate would not occur today among historians unless they took great care to define what was meant by the ideas of "fair" and "unfair" in a historical context. Question 4 seems a bit more promising. It could help you ask questions about the social dimensions of the law, a common approach for a historian.

Craft a Proposal

After you have completed your preliminary research, craft a one-page proposal. Your instructors and friends may be happy to read it and comment on it, but even if they are not, the process of writing the proposal will still help you sketch out your ideas. The proposal is an early opportunity to think critically about your topic.

The proposal should answer these questions:

1. What is your topic? Describe it briefly.
2. What is your hypothesis? Articulate the question that is driving your research, and what your tentative answer to this question is.
3. What will your readers learn from this project? Explain what new information your research will be bringing to light, or how you will be interpreting commonplace knowledge in a new way.
4. Why is your project significant or interesting? Discuss the relationship between your project and some broader issue in history.
5. What sources will you be using? Provide a list of books, articles, images, and other sources that will provide evidence.
6. What methods will you use to evaluate your sources? Tell what theoretical approaches you will be taking to

interpret your sources, or how you will be using methods from another discipline, such as sociology or anthropology, to inform your interpretation.

Write an Annotated Bibliography

Your objective for the next stage of your project should be to compile an **annotated bibliography**. This exercise will help you assess the breadth and significance of your sources. Arrange your sources according to the instructions for a bibliography given in Appendix B, "Citation Guide." After each entry in your bibliography, summarize the source and state why you will be using it in your paper. (For good examples of annotated bibliographies, see Oxford Bibliographies Online.) You should keep your notes on sources concise, but you may wish to say more about some sources than others; about 150 words will normally do for each entry. The summaries should address the following questions:

1. What type of source is it: a book, a journal article, a historical document?
2. What is the main argument or contribution of the source?
3. What evidence is presented by the source?
4. How is the source relevant to your research project?

Talk to People about Your Topic

Don't be bashful. It can be intimidating to seek out experts in your area of interest, but experts are usually happy to discuss specific research problems with other researchers, especially when they are presented with thoughtful questions and written proposals. If the experts happen to be history professors at your institution, visit them during their office hours, or make appointments to see them. You may also wish to seek out experts in other departments of a university, and outside of universities, too.

If You Have to Abandon a Topic, Do It Early

The process of finding sources, forming a hypothesis, and crafting a proposal will test the viability of your topic. If at the end of a week or two you no longer want to work on your topic, then choose another one. There are plenty of reasons to stop working on a topic: you may not find enough sources, or you may decide that the topic is less interesting than you thought. It is better to bail out of an unfeasible project early than to go down in flames later.

Review

1. Find a topic that interests you.
2. Visit your library.
3. Read bibliographies and footnotes to find more sources.
4. Make sure your sources are appropriate.
5. Read to develop a hypothesis and craft a proposal.

Notes

1. Alfred W. Crosby, Jr., *The Columbian Exchange: Biological and Cultural Consequences of 1492*, 30th Anniversary Edition (Westport: Praeger, 2003); Theodore Binnema, *Common and Contested Ground: A Human and Environmental History of the Northwestern Plains* (Norman: University of Oklahoma Press, 2001).

2. Andrew C. Isenberg, ed., *The Oxford Handbook of Environmental History* (Oxford: Oxford University Press, 2014).

3. James W. Daschuk, *Clearing the Plains: Disease, Politics of Starvation, and the Loss of Aboriginal Life* (Regina: University of Regina Press, 2013).

4. Daschuk, *Clearing the Plains*, 97–98.

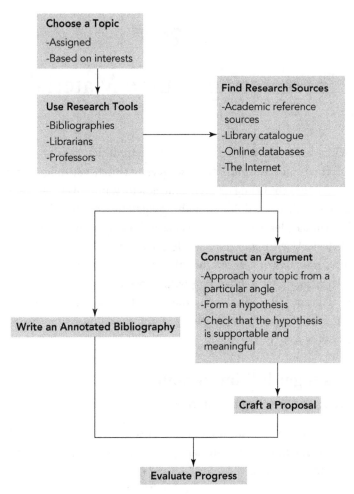

Flowchart Chapter 1   Constructing an argument based on sources

Interpreting Source Materials

When you write history, you will have to decide how to select, interpret, and assemble your sources. At first, you might find the sources confusing or even contradictory, but this is probably a sign that you are doing something right: the complexities of the human past leave us with a diverse and messy array of evidence. Historical writing resembles detective work because sources often raise more questions than they answer. Sometimes they lead historians on an exhilarating wild-goose chase that culminates in a dead end. Other times they enable historians to recover unexpected tales from the past. Fortunately, there are many ways to assess source materials.

Distinguish Primary Sources from Secondary Sources

Sources drive all histories, but not all sources are created equal. One distinction that historians make is between primary and secondary sources.

1.   **Primary Sources.** Primary sources originate in the time and place that historians are studying. They take many forms, including personal memoirs and correspondence, government documents, transcripts of legal proceedings, oral histories and traditions, archaeological and biological evidence, and visual sources such as paintings and photographs. Primary sources are the raw data of history, and fundamental to any good historical investigation.

Each kind of primary source must be considered on its own terms. Historians used to think that some types of sources were inherently more reliable than others. Leopold von Ranke, the founder of modern, professional history, considered government documents to be the gold standard of all primary sources. But even government documents are subjective in certain respects. Like all sources, they reveal some things but remain silent on others, and so it is important for you to think carefully, not just about the author and purpose of every source, but also about its intended audience. Was the creator of the source directly involved in what the source is describing? Why was the source produced, and what effect was it supposed to have?

Every primary source has potential value to the historian. The challenge is to find the right question to ask of the source. Be aware of a source's strengths and limitations, and take these into account when deciding how to use the source in your research.

2. Secondary Sources. Secondary sources reflect on earlier times. Typically, they are created by writers who are interpreting primary sources to make sense of the past. Secondary sources vary a great deal, from books by professional scholars to journalistic accounts in newspapers or on blogs to television programs and videos online. Evaluate each secondary source on its own merits. Pay particular attention to how well it uses primary sources as evidence, and to how extensively it engages with other secondary sources.

Not everyone who writes about history is a trained historian, and not every secondary source is equally reliable for academic research. Focus on using scholarly sources. Scholarly books and articles are written for an academic audience and go through a rigorous process of editing and peer review. They are based on original research, will clearly display their use of sources by providing copious references in the form of **citations,** and are designed to inform rather than entertain. Popular works of history, by contrast, are designed to interest or amuse general readers. Some are written by excellent historians and present fascinating accounts. Because they have not been checked as carefully as scholarly publications, however, they are simply not as suitable for your research. Look for secondary sources that have been written by experts and published by an academic press. Make sure that the writing is objective and that claims are supported with references to primary and secondary sources. Beware of articles published in so-called "predatory" journals that charge large fees to authors without providing rigorous editorial standards. When in doubt about the credibility of a secondary source, whether in print or online, ask your professor or check whether historians have referenced it in their research. If you come across a work of popular history that makes a claim you would like to pursue further, try to find a scholarly source on the same topic. Perhaps the author of the popular work has also written a more scholarly version, or has drawn upon careful academic research that you can then use in your own work.

There are some circumstances in which the common distinction between primary and secondary sources becomes blurred. The first possible area of confusion comes from using modern editions of historical texts. These are basically primary sources, but editors and translators may impart secondary source characteristics to them. Imagine that you are writing a paper on the Spanish conquest of the Aztecs in the sixteenth century. The letters of Hernán Cortés are an important primary source, because Cortés wrote these letters at the time (the 1520s) and in the place (Mexico) that you are studying. Depending on where you find these letters, however, there may be certain aspects of them that should not be considered a primary source: the editor's introduction and footnotes are secondary sources, because they were written after the events themselves. Furthermore, if your version of these letters is in English, then the words that you are reading are different from what was first written by Cortés. At the undergraduate level, translation does not in and of itself invalidate a source's status as a primary source, but you should be aware that someone other than the author is mediating between you and the original text. Choose a reliable edition with a well-respected translator, which can be verified by a quick check of whether expert scholars in the field use this version for their research and teaching. The words on the page won't be exactly the same as what the author wrote, but the essential points should remain the same. Exercise caution when basing any argument on exact wording unless you are willing to go back to the original words—and language—of the author.

A second possible area of confusion when trying to distinguish different kinds of sources arises when a secondary source shifts into the category of primary source. With the passage of time, the writings of a historian (normally secondary sources) may become primary source evidence for the historian's own historical context. One of the most famous books about the Spanish and the Aztecs is William H. Prescott's *History of the Conquest of Mexico*. First published in 1843, this book was clearly written after the events it describes. It is a classic secondary source that has been influential for generations of scholars who have built on it and overturned some of its conclusions. Because it is now considered out of date in many of its presumptions, it is not the best source to tell you about the Spanish and the Aztecs in the sixteenth century; it is, however, an excellent source to tell you about what Americans in the mid-nineteenth century thought about the Spanish and the Aztecs. In other words, it is a secondary source about Mexico in the sixteenth century (the subject of the book), and a primary source about the United States in the nineteenth century (the place and time of the book's composition).

Conduct Interviews Systematically

Interviewing people can be one of the most exciting aspects of historical research. If you are asked to conduct an interview for one of your courses, this opportunity can bring a sense of immediacy to research and writing. An interview is more than just a conversation: it is a way to seek critical information about the past, and you should be as systematic as possible in your interviewing. Here are some guidelines.

1. **Do Your Homework.** Before you conduct the interview, learn what you can from written sources. Then make a list of questions that you want to ask your subject. If you do not know some basic information about your history, you will waste your time and your subject's. Your subject will also think you do not know what you are talking about and will not trust you.

2. **Be Considerate.** Tell your subjects about your project and ask for permission to quote. They may only be willing to share information with you anonymously. You must respect their wishes because their position may be more delicate than you think. If you are a student, your university may also have published ethical guidelines for conducting research with other people as subjects. There may even be laws about "human subjects" in your jurisdiction. Ask your instructor if this is the case, and be sure to follow the guidelines. If you are a graduate student, a postdoctoral researcher, or a faculty member, you will almost certainly be obliged to follow your university's standards for research on human subjects. All warnings aside, you will find that many people enjoy being interviewed for a history; it can be very flattering to know that one's experiences have been historically significant.

3. **Be Patient.** It takes time to interview people, and it may even be difficult to get in touch with some subjects. Often you will find it is a good idea to have references, or to mail your potential subject a résumé and a brief description of your project. It might also take two or three interviews before your subject trusts you enough to share interesting information with you. If you plan to interview people, therefore, start work early so that you can meet your deadlines.

4. Take Scrupulous Notes. Always take written notes during an interview. You may also want to use a digital recorder or smartphone app, but batteries can die and the wrong buttons can get pressed. Back up your work with written notes. Technical problems happen, but they are not the only problems with recorded notes. A recording gives you a more accurate record of the interview, but use of a recorder can also frighten your subjects. If you notice that the recording device is interfering with the interview, shut it off.

5. Think Critically about Oral Sources. Like any other source, interviews should be subject to critical evaluation. Be aware that your subjects provide their own unique perspective. If it is possible, compare their stories with the stories that other people tell you, and also compare oral sources with any available written sources. Written sources are not necessarily more reliable than oral sources, but writing preserves its own version of history and should be considered alongside oral history whenever possible.

6. Cultivate Your Skills as an Interviewer and as an Interpreter of Interviews. It takes a lot of practice to learn how to work with sources, and interviewing is no different. The best interviewers are usually the most experienced. There are also a number of good guides to interviewing. For a formal introduction, see Donald Ritchie's book *Doing Oral History: A Practical Guide*.[1] Excellent resources may be found online at the website of the Oral History Association, http://www.oralhistory.org, and in the "Smithsonian Folklife and Oral History Interviewing Guide," which can be downloaded free from https://folklife.si.edu/education#resources.

Consider Visual and Material Sources

Most academic historians have traditionally focused on written sources, but many, including historians of science and technology, archaeologists, and art historians, do work frequently with images and objects. Images and objects can give you new perspectives on things, but it is not always easy to analyze them historically. Try to follow these guidelines, borrowed from an article by Jules Prown called "Mind in Matter,"[2] which are common methods used across the disciplines to analyze images and materials.

1. **Describe the Image or Object.** What can you observe in the source itself? Give a physical description of the object, or of the image and the things that are portrayed. How is it shaped? If you can measure it, what are its dimensions (size, weight)? If you cannot measure it, estimate the dimensions. Can you find any obvious symbols on the object, such as markings, decorations, or inscriptions?

2. **Think about the Image or Object.** In the case of an image, how does it compare to other images? Does it have patterns and shapes that are similar to or different from other images? Does it contain recognizable styles? For an object, what is it like to interact with it? What does it feel like? When you use the object, do you have to take into account its size, weight, or shape? What does the object do, and how does it do it? Does it work well? What is it like to use it? How do you feel about using this object? Do you like it? Does it frustrate you? Is it puzzling?

3. **Make an Argument about the Image or Object.** Can you analyze this source imaginatively and plausibly? Review your descriptions and deductions. What sorts of hypotheses can you make? Can you make a historically significant argument about the image or object? What might it have been like for someone to see this image or to use this object in the past? Use other sources as a lens for interpreting the image or object. What other evidence can you use to test your hypotheses, speculations, and deductions?

Refine Your Hypothesis

While you are examining each source, you should be asking how it might support or contradict your hypothesis. Pretty soon, you will have a lot of information that relates to your research question. If you aren't sure how to organize it, try arranging your answers as would a reporter.

Historian Richard Marius began his career as a journalist, and in his *Short Guide to Writing about History* he advises students to ask the reporter's questions of "who," "what," "why," "where," and "when" as they read source materials. It is good advice. Answers to these questions can be very complex, depending on the sources and the story.[3] Imagine for a moment that you are writing an essay about Marie de l'Incarnation, an Ursuline nun in New France, and that your sources consist mainly of seventeenth-century texts. To get through these sources, you have formed a hypothesis: that Marie's ability to attract donations was critical to the survival of the Ursuline convent in seventeenth-century Quebec. Now organize your research around the reporter's questions, and take note of the answers.

The *Who* Question. Historians ask "who" to learn biographical information about significant actors, to learn who bore the brunt of historical changes, and to learn who caused things to happen. In your essay on Marie de l'Incarnation, you could use the sources to make yourself familiar with all the main characters. Who were Marie's family members, and did they shape her decisions? Who supported Marie when she went to New France? Who opposed her? Who were the donors to the Ursuline convent? Who were the sharpest critics of the institution?

The *What* Question. Different sources often describe the same events differently. Know each version of events so that you can compare accounts. What did Marie say in her letters about donations to the convent? Did she say different things to different people? What do the financial accounts of the institution record? What were people outside the convent saying about the institution's poverty?

The *Why* Question. Historians often ask why some things changed while other things remained the same. Using each source, make a list of possible causes. Try to distinguish the most significant causes of events from the background causes. Why did the Ursuline convent in Quebec struggle so much financially? Were some of the sources exaggerating or understating the level of poverty? If so, what reasons might the authors have had for presenting the convent's wealth in such a way? Why did people donate to the convent? Did it depend on their relationships with the people in the community including Marie de l'Incarnation? Why were some of the convent's neighbours, both Indigenous people and French settlers, more supportive of its goals than others?

The *Where* Question. Sometimes you will find fairly self-evident answers to the *where* question. Other times, geographical considerations will open your eyes to unexpected circumstances. You might even find it helpful to draw a map of your subject. Where, for example, did the donations to the Ursuline convent come from? Are there patterns on either side of the Atlantic that you can discern? Given the large distances between New France and France, and the time it took for a shipment to reach the convent from across the Atlantic, were some food donations more suitable than others?

The *When* Question. Historians analyze change and continuity over time. Not surprisingly, it can become quite important to know exactly when historical events happened. Depending on the topic, you may get an easy answer to the *when* question or no answer at all. Try as much as you can to determine when things happened, and use this information to place events in a chronological relationship. You may want to make one timeline from all your source materials so that you better understand the order of events. When, for example, was the convent in the most dire of financial straits? Did this coincide with actions by Marie de l'Incarnation? How did the pattern of donations change after particularly difficult hardships like a fire in the convent or an especially bad winter?

You will not always find answers to all these questions, and the answers that you do find will not always be immediately relevant to your main research question. Do not be distressed about this. Searching for evidence and asking the questions will help you think about the sources and what they mean.

Be Sensitive to Points of View in Your Sources

As you use your hypothesis to work your way through the source materials, you will come to see that each source presents history from a particular point of view. Many students perceive this as "bias" and become immediately inclined to dismiss the source, but good historians understand that every source has a perspective. Even photographs show only the perspective of the photographer. Photographers have even been known to arrange their pictures so as to "edit" the overall story being told, and their mere presence with a camera changes how their subjects behave. How then do historians know which sources to trust? They use good judgment in assessing reliability, and they remain mindful of how sources came to be produced.

Knowing how a source became available can illuminate why only some information is presented. Chroniclers record events as they happen, but they describe only the things they consider to be important. In a book called *Silencing the Past*, Michel-Rolph Trouillot explains that Caribbean slave owners usually kept detailed records of their plantations, but points out that sometimes the slave owners neglected to record births. Infant mortality was so high on some plantations that it was not worth the trouble to add a new slave child to the registers until the baby survived to a certain age. Therefore, these records lack important data. Historians may wish to reconstruct the history of Caribbean slave families, but the plantation records render the task difficult. People use their own contemporary standards when they decide to record certain events and to keep silent about others, and their decisions should be borne in mind by historians when assessing how reliable the source is.[4]

The process of producing sources does not end with the selections of the first creators. All sorts of factors determine whether or not sources will survive. Sometimes wars, fires, and floods can silence the past. But most of the time, collectors, archivists, and librarians decide to preserve some sources and to discard others. They have their own visions of the past, and politics and economics can influence their decisions in many ways. For example, during the 1960s Loren Graham began to collect information about a Soviet engineer named Peter Palchinsky, who was executed by Stalin in 1929. Graham believed that Palchinsky had made significant contributions to early Soviet engineering, but the Soviet government was hiding Palchinsky's papers from researchers because the engineer had criticized the regime. Graham had to wait almost thirty years, but when the Soviet Union collapsed he finally gained access to Palchinsky's papers. Then, in a nice twist of fate, Graham found that the papers could help him write a book that explained, in part, the Soviet Union's failure. His quest for sources became a subplot of his history *The Ghost of the Executed Engineer*.[5]

Select the Most Important Source Materials

You cannot include everything in your essay, and in selecting the information that you need to make your point, you will sometimes need to forego potentially interesting tangents. Historians are not just collectors of facts; they are selectors and arrangers. Try not to be like the main character in Jorge Luis Borges's story "Funes, the Memorious":

> He remembered the shapes of the clouds in the south at dawn on the 30th of April of 1882, and he could compare them

in his recollection with the marbled grain in the design of a leather-bound book which he had seen only once, and with the lines in the spray which an oar raised in the Rio Negro on the eve of the battle of Quebracho. . . . He told me . . . My memory, sir, is like a garbage disposal.[6]

Historians exercise selectivity with sources so that they avoid producing garbage disposals. Some information will be significant to an essay, but much will not. Don't feel bad if you spend a lot of time interpreting a source, only to find that it does not contribute to your essay's main idea. Although is tempting to include such sources, if only to show your readers how hard you have been working, a coherent essay will impress readers more than a garbage disposal. If you cannot bear to part with interesting but irrelevant information, move it to a separate file for deployment in a future project.

Take Notes by Being Selective

When you first begin to analyze your sources, you will need to take notes. When historians take notes, they employ a number of techniques: some use index cards and notebook paper, while others use word-processing or database programs. Choosing a method depends to a great extent on the type of research you are conducting, and it is often a matter of personal preference. As you conduct more research, you will get a better sense of how you prefer to take notes.

All note-taking methods, whether low-tech or high-tech, present a common difficulty: how to select the most important material for your notes. Usually, you do not want to copy your sources word for word; you want to write down only the information that is likely to be useful in your essay. But how do you know what is going to be useful before you even write a **draft**? Reaching this decision is the most difficult part of note-taking. You would like to record useful information, but you recognize that some apparently useless information may turn out to be useful later.

Because it is difficult to know in advance which notes will be useful, you should use your hypothesis to help you read sources. Ask yourself how a source relates to your main ideas, and jot down notes from the source that answer the fundamental questions about your hypothesis. In using your hypothesis to help select the most important information from your sources, don't ignore or neglect information that contradicts or challenges your hypothesis: this information will be important when you account for **counterarguments**.

Indeed, the trickiest thing about using a hypothesis during note-taking is that your hypothesis is likely to change as your research progresses. This is as it should be. Over the course of your research, you will refine your ideas about your sources, and your hypothesis will get closer and closer to a **thesis** or argument. Unfortunately, this also means that your early notes will be more extensive and less useful than your later notes. Don't be disappointed if, at the end of a project, you find that you have taken some extraneous notes; it is a natural consequence of refining a hypothesis and being selective. Remember that you can always return to these notes later if you decide to take your research in a new direction. And if you find as you proceed that information from your sources diverges more and more from your hypothesis, it is better to change your hypothesis than to disregard your sources: good historians adjust their arguments to remain true to the evidence.

Review

1. Think as you read.
2. Question your sources.
3. Be aware of sources' perspectives.
4. Take notes that are relevant to your hypothesis.

Notes

1. Donald Ritchie, *Doing Oral History: A Practical Guide* (New York: Oxford University Press, 2014).
2. Jules David Prown, "Mind in Matter: An Introduction to Material Culture Theory and Method," in *Material Life in America, 1600–1860*, ed. Robert Blair St. George (Boston: Northeastern University Press, 1991), 17–35. Thanks to Elizabeth Abrams for suggesting this article.
3. For a broader discussion of these research questions, see Richard Marius, *A Short Guide to Writing about History*, 2nd ed. (New York: HarperCollins, 1995), 33–43.
4. Michel-Rolph Trouillot, *Silencing the Past: Power and the Production of History* (Boston: Beacon Press, 1995), 49–53.
5. Loren R. Graham, *The Ghost of the Executed Engineer: Technology and the Fall of the Soviet Union* (Cambridge, MA: Harvard University Press, 1993).
6. Jorge Luis Borges, *Ficciones*, trans. Emecé Editores (New York: Grove Press, 1962), 112.

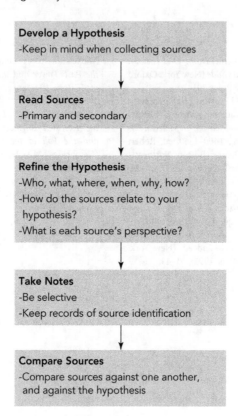

Flowchart Chapter 2   Taking notes

3

Writing History Faithfully

In the first century BCE, Cicero said, "The first law for the historian is that he shall never dare utter an untruth. The second is that he shall suppress nothing that is true."[1] The spirit of these laws remains the same, even if some of the conventions for writing history have changed—such as the present convention, unobserved by Cicero or his translator, for writing in language that is gender-inclusive.

Good historical writers always question authorities, even formidable ones like Cicero. So how do historians know what is true? They may never know the full answer to such a question because sources often present contradictions and silences. Even so, historians recognize certain rules of representing the past faithfully. These rules are subject to variation and reinterpretation over time, yet a broad consensus nevertheless exists among historical writers about what is right and what is wrong.

Collect and Report Your Sources Carefully

There is more to honesty than simply having good intentions. Historians have the responsibility of speaking for the past, and therefore it is essential that they report accurately on the people and events of the past. All scholars build on the work of others. Historians need to be able to trust that other historians have been faithful to their sources.

Careless reading and sloppy note-taking can lead you to misrepresent history. Even if your misrepresentations are inadvertent, readers may still accuse you of dishonesty. To avoid any such misunderstanding, apply some basic rules to your note-taking:

1. **Include a Citation with Every Note.** Each and every time you jot down a note, write the bibliographic reference next to it. Every note card, computer entry, and piece of paper should indicate where you got the information. Always include page numbers. If you are pressed for time, do not cut corners in your notes; work out a system of abbreviations. This will help later, too, when you may need to look back for a specific quote that suits your argument.

2. **Distinguish Clearly Between Your Words and Your Source's Words.** Always put direct quotations in quotation marks. When you paraphrase or summarize someone else's words, make sure that your own words are distinct.

3. **Watch Your Word Processor.** Ages ago, when historians wrote with quill pens or typewriters, writing and revising drafts was a painful process. The smallest alterations made it necessary to rewrite or retype the entire manuscript. Nowadays, word processing makes it easier to compose and revise while you consult sources. This is convenient, but presents some organizational challenges. Always keep your notes in a separate file from your writing. Be especially careful when cutting and pasting source materials from the Internet. If you keep notes and text in the same file, you run the risk of confusing your own words with someone else's.

4. **Consider Using Online Organizers.** Increasingly, historians are turning to online project management software to organize research and note-taking. There are several types of software available, and one program has been developed with historians in mind. The Center for History and New Media at George Mason University has created a program called

Zotero, which helps historians collect, organize, and cite their sources. The program plugs into conventional web-browsing and word-processing software and is available for free at http://www.zotero.org.

Treat the Ideas of Others with Care and Respect

When you conduct research and write papers, you will have to engage the ideas of fellow scholars. Much of the time you will be interpreting subjects that others have interpreted before you. Even if you are the first person to write a history of something, you will have to place your own ideas in the context of a broader historical literature to show the significance of your contribution.

All historians know that writing is hard work. Therefore, it is important to acknowledge the work of others respectfully. Historians have conventions for quoting, summarizing, and paraphrasing the works of other scholars. If you follow these conventions at the note-taking stage, you won't have to go back and check your sources again while you are writing.

Know the Difference between Paraphrases and Summaries

Technically speaking, a **paraphrase** restates what someone has written by using about the same number of words as in the original, whereas a **summary** uses fewer words. Paraphrase when you would like to discuss someone else's work but you think you can say the same thing more clearly in your own words for the purposes of your paper. Summarize when you can capture the essential points in a shorter form.

In historical writing, paraphrasing is not as common as summarizing, but it still has its uses. A paraphrase can be particularly helpful when you want to render an archaic or complex quotation into standard English. For example, in *To Keep and Bear Arms: The Origins of an Anglo-American Right*, historian Joyce Malcolm analyzes passages from William Blackstone's *Commentaries on the Laws of England*, the eighteenth century's most famous interpretation of the law. Blackstone wrote, "In a land of liberty, it is extremely dangerous to make a distinct order of the profession of arms." Malcolm precedes this slightly archaic quotation with her own paraphrase: "As for standing armies, Blackstone recommended they be treated with utmost caution."[2] Malcolm's paraphrase helps readers understand Blackstone's somewhat old-fashioned terminology.

A summary of someone else's work is usually more convenient than a paraphrase because historians write to express their own original ideas, even when they are engaging the ideas of others. Summaries are particularly useful when you want to synthesize the ideas of others and present them in concise form. In a collection of articles entitled *The Conquest of Acadia, 1710*, Maurice Basque briefly summarizes the work of John Bartlet Brebner (1895–1957), the historian who coined the term "North Atlantic Triangle":

> Generations of historians have been influenced by John Bartlet Brebner's reading of Acadians' reaction to military and political events, specifically that Acadian society was not politically minded.

Basque then summarizes some of Brebner's evidence and discusses his influence on the work of other historians. He also provides citations for further exploration.[3]

Both summaries and paraphrases indicate to the reader that you have grasped someone else's idea firmly enough that you are able to convey it in your own words. In either case, be sure to include all the relevant points made in the original passage, and also make sure to show that this is indeed a fair summary or paraphrase, not a presentation of your own ideas.

Learn How and When to Quote

Historians usually demonstrate their familiarity with sources by summarizing and paraphrasing, but occasionally they find that a direct quotation is the best way to make a point. Use a direct quotation when the language of your source is vivid and you cannot possibly do it justice with summary or paraphrase, or when your interpretation depends on the exact wording of the original. Otherwise, try to limit your use of quotations. Your audience is reading your writing principally to find out your own original ideas. Too many quotations can leave the your audience confused about where your own original ideas are, or wondering whether you have grasped the main points and important ideas in your research. An overuse of quotation can also make for a very bumpy read, as the reader is jostled repeatedly between your words and the words of your sources.

There are two ways to incorporate quotations. Most of the time when historians quote, they run a short quotation into their own text. This is most effective when the sentence smoothly joins an identification of the source with the quotation itself. You can begin the sentence by telling the reader who is speaking, and then insert the quotation. If you were writing about the nineteenth-century French philosopher Pierre-Joseph Proudhon, for instance, you could write the following:

> At a time when the French middle classes were growing, Proudhon was quite brave to declare that "property is theft."

A citation would be placed at the end of the sentence to indicate where you found the Proudhon quote. Notice that the body of the sentence is not separated from the quotation by a comma or a colon. These punctuation marks should be used only when the grammatical structure of the sentence requires it:

> As Proudhon bravely declared at a time when the French middle classes were growing, "property is theft."

The second kind of quotation is called a **block quotation**. When it is necessary to quote a passage that is longer than three lines, indent five spaces from the left and right margins and type the quotation in a block set off from the text. The sentence before the quotation should introduce it; the sentence after the quotation should link it to the text that follows. For example, in his pioneering social history *The Making of the English Working Class*, E.P. Thompson used block quotations to give readers a flavour of English discourse on the subject of labour during the late eighteenth and early nineteenth centuries. To define some key terms, he used the words of the activist Francis Place. Thompson wrote:

> Such diversity of experiences has led some writers to question both the notions of an "industrial revolution" and of a "working class." The first discussion need not detain us here. The term is serviceable enough in its usual connotations. For the second, many writers prefer the term working classes, which emphasises the great disparity in status, acquisitions, skills, conditions within the portmanteau phrase. And in this they echo the complaints of Francis Place:
>
> > If the character and the conduct of the working people are to be taken from reviews, magazines, pamphlets, newspapers, reports of the two Houses of Parliament and the Factory Commissioners, we shall find them all jumbled together as the "lower orders," the most skilled and the most prudent workman, with the most ignorant and imprudent laborers and paupers, though the difference is great indeed, and indeed in many cases will scarce admit of comparison.
>
> Place is, of course, right: the Sunderland tailor, the Irish navvy, the Jewish costermonger, the inmate of an East Anglian village workhouse, the compositor on *The Times*—all might be seen by their "betters" as belonging to the "lower classes"

while they themselves might scarcely understand each other's dialect.[4]

Thompson uses the quotation as a vivid illustration of a point, and connects his own ideas to the ideas of Place by seamlessly joining the block quotation to the preceding and following paragraphs. If you are going to include quotations in your writing, follow the same pattern. Use them sparingly lest they lose their force, and combine them with your own analysis of the words' significance to your essay.

Use Ellipses and Brackets, but Do Justice to Your Sources

When historians insert a quotation into their writing, they can abridge or alter it gently so that it fits more snugly into their own material. They indicate these changes with **ellipses**, which look like three periods and indicate that something has been removed, and with square brackets, which indicate that something has been added or changed. If you were going to quote the previous sentence but alter it gently, you could write it like this: "[Historians] indicate these changes with ellipses . . . and with square brackets." The square brackets around the word "Historians" tell readers that this word was not in the original text but has been supplied by the person using the quotation, and the ellipses between "ellipses" and "and with square brackets" indicate that the original contained more text there than what has been reproduced in the quotation. One basic rule governs the use of ellipses and brackets: any abridged or altered quotation must be faithful to the original, full quotation. It would not be a fair use of these symbols if you were to write "[Bad writers] indicate these . . . ellipses, which look like . . . square brackets," because this sentence means something fundamentally different from the original.

Marks of ellipsis and brackets are not always easy to use well. Imagine that you are writing a short essay about the "Declaration of Independence." You have decided to analyze Thomas Jefferson's complaints about how King George III treated the American colonial legislatures. Jefferson enumerated these complaints:

- He has refused his Assent to Laws, the most wholesome and necessary for the Public Good.
- He has forbidden his Governors to pass laws of immediate and pressing importance, unless suspended in their operation till his Assent should be obtained; and when so suspended, he has utterly neglected to attend to them.
- He has refused to pass other Laws for the accommodation of large districts of people, unless those people would relinquish the right of Representation in the Legislature, a right inestimable to them and formidable to tyrants only.
- He has called together legislative bodies at places unusual, uncomfortable, and distant from the depository of their Public Records, for the sole purpose of fatiguing them into compliance with his measures.
- He has dissolved Representative Houses repeatedly, for opposing with manly firmness his invasions on the rights of the people.
- He has refused for a long time, after such dissolutions, to cause others to be elected; whereby the Legislative Powers, incapable of Annihilation, have returned to the People at large for their exercise; the State remaining in the meantime exposed to all the dangers of invasion from without, and convulsions within.

Jefferson's language is unique and vivid; therefore you wish to use quotations to support your point. But as much as you would like to quote Jefferson in full, it would take up too much space in a short essay. For this reason, you decide to convey Jefferson's main points by abridging his writing with marks of ellipsis:

Jefferson listed five complaints about the ways in which King George III treated the colonial legislatures: "He has refused his Assent to Laws. . . . He has forbidden his Governors to pass laws of immediate and pressing importance. . . . He has refused to pass other Laws for the accommodation of large districts of people. . . . He has called together legislative bodies at places unusual. . . . He has dissolved Representative Houses repeatedly. . . . He has refused for a long time . . . to cause others to be elected. . . ."

But notice that your sentence does not flow well into the quotation: there is a jarring difference between your verb tense and Jefferson's. You could eliminate the problem by removing the word "has," except that you would be stuck with the incorrect form of the verb "to forbid." In addition, writing "King George" and then having the quotation repeat "he" as the subject sounds unnatural. To solve these problems, you may wish to insert some bracketed words so that your sentence flows naturally into the quotation from Jefferson. The brackets say to your readers that these are not Jefferson's exact words, but they still convey Jefferson's exact meaning. You may decide to write:

Jefferson listed five complaints about how King George III treated the colonial legislatures, namely that he "refused his Assent to Laws . . . [forbade] his Governors to pass laws of immediate and pressing importance . . . refused to pass other Laws for the accommodation of large districts of people . . . called together legislative bodies at places un- usual . . . dissolved Representative Houses repeatedly . . . [and] refused for a long time . . . to cause others to be elected. . . . "

This quotation is faithful to Jefferson's exact meaning, even though it abridges his quotation with ellipses and brackets. It would have been unfaithful to use ellipses in this manner, for example: "He has refused to pass other Laws for the accommodation of large districts of people . . . for the sole purpose of fatiguing them into compliance with his measures." Such a use would be unfair to Jefferson, because the first portion of the original quotation was followed by an entirely different set of ideas: "unless those people would relinquish the right of Representation in the Legislature, a right inestimable to them and formidable to tyrants only."

It also would have been unfaithful to Jefferson to use brackets this way: "He has forbidden his Governors to pass [important] laws. . . ." This changes the sense of the original quotation, "He has forbidden his Governors to pass laws of immediate and pressing importance. . . ." If you need to be so concise, summarizing Jefferson in your own words would be preferable to inserting different words directly into Jefferson's original writing.

Place Quotation Marks Properly

After apostrophes, quotation marks probably cause more confusion than any other form of punctuation. This is partly because North American practice differs from British practice. Most of us probably read historical works from all over the English-speaking world, and so when it comes to your own writing you may indeed have grounds for confusion.

1. **North American Style for Quotation Marks.** When you run a quotation into your text, place the words of the quotation inside double quotation marks:

> Pierre Elliott Trudeau famously declared that "there's no place for the state in the bedrooms of the nation."

For a quotation within a quotation, use single quotation marks:

> In his biography of Pierre Elliott Trudeau, John English writes that the Justice minister "cleverly borrowed *Globe and Mail* editorialist Martin O'Malley's statement 'The state has no place in the bedrooms of the nation' and, in a December 22, 1967, television interview made it famously his own."[5]

Notice also how the other forms of punctuation are placed in relation to the quotation marks. Periods and commas should be placed *inside* them. If you use question marks and exclamation points, place these inside the quotation marks only when they form part of the original quotation. If you are adding your own question marks and exclamation points after the quotation, then place these outside the quotation marks. Colons and semicolons also go outside the quotation marks.

2. British Style for Quotation Marks. The British use quotation marks in the opposite way from North Americans. When a quotation is run into the text, the words of the quotation are placed in single quotation marks:

> Pierre Elliott Trudeau famously declared that 'there's no place for the state in the bedrooms of the nation'.

For a quotation within a quotation, double quotation marks are used:

> In his biography of Pierre Elliott Trudeau, John English writes that the Justice minister 'cleverly borrowed *Globe and Mail* editorialist Martin O'Malley's statement "The state has no place in the bedrooms of the nation" and, in a December 22, 1967, television interview made it famously his own'.[6]

Notice also that in British usage all other punctuation marks are placed *outside* the quotation marks.

Don't Plagiarize

Historians find unfaithful quotations disturbing, but they reserve the harshest condemnation for plagiarists. In the ancient Mediterranean world, *plagiarii* were pirates who kidnapped young children, among other misdeeds.[7] When plagiarists claim someone else's ideas as their own they steal someone else's brainchild. And contrary to folk wisdom, there is no honour among thieves. Historians do not tolerate plagiarists. Universities punish them.

Cases of **plagiarism** happen infrequently because there is such a powerful consensus against it. Historians share this commitment to honesty with writers in the academe across all the disciplines. It is so pleasurable to share ideas honestly and to write history faithfully that real historians should never feel an urge to plagiarize.

1.   **Direct Plagiarism.** Direct plagiarism occurs when one writer takes another writer's exact words and passes them off as his or her own. Direct plagiarism is very easy for an informed reader to spot. It is also very easy for the student to avoid: simply use quotation marks to indicate whenever you have used the exact words of one of your sources, and be sure to include a citation each time you get words or ideas from a source, whether you quote, paraphrase, or summarize.

2.   **Indirect Plagiarism.** Indirect plagiarism is more difficult to recognize and it is also more insidious. Indirect plagiarism occurs when a writer paraphrases someone else's work too closely. The basic structure of the sentence or paragraph is retained, and the plagiarist substitutes an occasional new word or phrase to make the writing slightly different. For example, here is an original passage taken from Thomas Holt's book about emancipated slaves in Jamaica, *The Problem of Freedom.* Holt writes:

> Presiding over this sparkling court was Elizabeth Vassall Fox, who had inherited her estates in 1800 from her grandfather Florentius Vassall. Yet Lady Holland was as staunch a Whig as her husband and shared many of his libertarian sentiments.[8]

The following passage is an overly close paraphrase that would be an example of indirect plagiarism, even if the author gave a citation to Holt, because the paraphrase is too close to Holt's original text to be considered the author's original writing:

> Elizabeth Vassall Fox had inherited her estates in 1800 from her grandfather. She presided over this sparkling court, yet was as staunch a Whig and a libertarian as her husband.

To avoid plagiarizing, use quotation marks around the phrases that you have copied word-for-word from the source, and rewrite the rest of the passage so that it is your own writing in words and structure.

3. Inadvertent Plagiarism. What if you accidentally forget to put quotation marks around a passage from someone else's writing? What if you forget to provide a citation when you summarize someone else's writing? Think for a minute about your audience. When they read your work, all they see are the words in front of them. They do not see how you were frantically putting your essay together at two in the morning. When they are reading your work, they presume that all the ideas and words in it are your own, unless indicated otherwise by the use of citations and quotation marks. By the time you tell them that you were in a rush and made some mistakes, they will not care. When your readers detect a misstep on your part, they will instinctively form a bad impression of your trustworthiness. Do not wait until the last minute to research and write historical essays. Be sure that there is plenty of time to document historical sources correctly.

4. Academic Dishonesty. Plagiarism means you are passing off someone else's work as your own. Therefore, it should go without saying that you should not submit an essay that someone else wrote for you. Do not submit a paper that you have bought from an essay-writing company or that you received from a friend. If you do these things you are a plagiarist because someone else did the work for which you are earning credit.

There are other acts of academic dishonesty that closely resemble plagiarism. Submitting the same paper in two courses without the prior permission of both instructors means you are passing off work done in one course as work done in another course and earning twice the credit for half the work. An instructor's permission is usually also required if you want to submit a paper that you wrote in collaboration with another student. It is usually appropriate for you to discuss a paper assignment with another student, but when it comes to writing, do it alone.

Cite Accurately

It is conceivable that after reading the preceding section on plagiarism and dishonesty, you will be so frightened that you will provide a citation in every sentence you write. Don't go overboard with citations. Include a citation when you quote directly, when you paraphrase or summarize someone else's ideas, or when you are consciously imitating the structure of someone else's writing. There is no need to give a citation for a piece of information that reasonable people consider to be general knowledge— for example, that the Allies landed at Normandy on June 6, 1944, or that the Mediterranean Sea lies between Africa and Europe. These pieces of information should be obvious to everyone who has studied history. Of course, if you are unsure whether something is common knowledge, play it safe and offer a citation.

All scholars agree to use sources responsibly. Two principles underlie all **citation systems**: they should be used consistently, and they should make it easy for your readers to check your sources. There is less agreement among scholars about specific methods for citing source materials. Some publishers and editors may require special citation formats, and some professors may have special requirements, too. For this reason it is important for historians to find out which format their audience expects them to use.

Students sometimes find citing sources to be confusing, because history instructors often have different rules from those in other disciplines. For example, many social scientists use the APA system, and many scholars of literature use the MLA system, where an author's name, date of publication, and page number are placed in parentheses after a quotation, summary, or paraphrase. Sometimes historians find these systems suit an essay or book particularly well. Nevertheless, most historians and history instructors favour sequential footnotes or **endnotes**, using what is called the Chicago system, because these are the easiest form for the reader to use when looking for the writer's sources. You can find a full guide to this system in *The Chicago Manual of Style*, and a shorter version of the same rules in Kate L. Turabian's *A Manual for Writers of Term Papers, Theses, and Dissertations*.[9] Both of these publications can be found in any academic library. Keep in mind that if you choose Zotero software to manage your research and note-taking, it will automatically format all your notes for you, but you should still check the notes to make sure that they are formatted correctly. For further guidance on exactly how to format footnotes, endnotes, and bibliographies, please see "Appendix B: Citation Guide."

Review

1. Record and report your sources with care.
2. When you quote, paraphrase, or summarize someone else's work, do so fairly.
3. Use the appropriate citation system, and cite your sources every time you present information from them, whether through direct quotation, paraphrase, or summary.
4. Don't forget the bibliography.

Notes

1. Cicero, *Pro Publio Sestio*, 2.62. As quoted by John Bartlett and Justin Kaplan, eds., *Bartlett's Familiar Quotations*, 16th ed. (Boston: Little, Brown, 1992), 87.

2. Joyce Lee Malcolm, *To Keep and Bear Arms: The Origins of an Anglo-American Right* (Cambridge, MA: Harvard University Press, 1994), 143.

3. Maurice Basque, "Family and Political Culture in Pre-Conquest Acadia," in *The Conquest of Acadia, 1710*, John G. Reid, Maurice Basque, Elizabeth Mancke, Barry Moody, Geoffrey Plank, and William Wicken (Toronto: University of Toronto Press, 2004), 49.

4. E.P. Thompson, *The Making of the English Working Class* (New York: Vintage Books, 1963; pbk. ed. 1966), 193–94.

5. John English, *Citizen of the World: The Life of Pierre Elliott Trudeau* (Toronto: A.A. Knopf, 2006), 447.

6. English, *Citizen of the World*, 447.

7. Harvey, *Writing with Sources*, 21–23.

8. Thomas C. Holt, *The Problem of Freedom: Race, Labor, and Politics in Jamaica, 1832–1938* (Baltimore: Johns Hopkins University Press, 1992), 83.

9. Kate L. Turabian, *A Manual for Writers of Term Papers, Theses, and Dissertations*, 8th ed. (Chicago: University of Chicago Press, 2013).

4

Using Sources to Make Inferences

It is impossible to know exactly what happened in the past, but this has not stopped people from writing about it. Walt Whitman wrote in *Specimen Days* that the "interior history" of the United States Civil War "will not only never be written—its practicality, minutiae of deeds and passions, will never be even suggested."[1] That may be so, but Whitman still tried to interpret the Civil War. He did so by making reasoned inferences.

An **inference** is more than just a hunch. It is an intelligent conclusion based on examination and comparison of evidence. When Whitman examined the wounded soldiers in an army hospital, he concluded that the Civil War was indescribably brutal. Whitman wrote this about the war, and people believed him, even though the poet had not seen every casualty and every battlefield. He had seen enough wounded men to build a moving argument. Like Whitman, historians also suggest probable interpretations by using their sources to make inferences.

What is it, then, that makes an inferential argument interesting and persuasive? Good writers make inferences by juxtaposing sources in a new, provocative way. At a time when people on both sides, North and South, were mobilizing armies to kill and maim each other, Whitman recognized that it would take more than pacifist principles to turn public opinion against the war. He hoped that by taking evidence that he saw in the army hospital, and building this evidence through inference into an argument, he might change the way people thought about the war. New evidence, or a new approach to old evidence, can call into question the received wisdom of the day.

Inferential reasoning is based on thoughtful comparison. When historians write about the past, they assess source materials by cross-checking information. Historians never read sources alone. Even when they have just one source on a given subject, they will read it in the context of their own general knowledge, and they will compare it with other sources to help them better understand its evidence.

Be True to Recognized Facts

All inferences begin with a consideration of the facts. Some facts are easy to recognize, but occasionally you may encounter people who are unduly skeptical about recognized facts. Good historians probe factual uncertainties, but they do not invent convenient facts and they do not ignore inconvenient facts.

Transform Facts into Evidence

There is more to writing history than just gathering facts and arranging them into some sort of order. A fact, merely by its existence, does not prove anything. Facts take on meaning when we examine and interpret them. As John H. Arnold remarks, historians try to create an interesting, coherent and useful narrative about the past. The past itself is not a narrative; in its entirety, it is as chaotic, uncoordinated, and complex as life. History is about making sense of that mess, finding or creating patterns and meanings and stories from the maelstrom.[2] Historians wade into the maelstrom to seek out the most reliable information, and then do their best to determine its accuracy before they use it to make inferences.

Investigate Your Facts

Sometimes the facts are not what they seem, and it is not always easy to discern where "the facts" stop and interpretation starts.

In Canada, for instance, the 1990s were a period of intense debate on the rights of First Nations, Inuit, and Métis peoples. The historical geographer Cole Harris, recognizing that the size of pre-contact Indigenous populations in British Columbia could have some bearing on issues such as land claims, also recognized that both Indigenous and non-Indigenous estimates could be influenced by political and economic considerations. Therefore, he set out to determine accurate figures. He did not simply accept any of the claims being made at the time, nor did he accept that it was impossible so many years later to determine the population size. Instead, Harris gathered all the data he could find, examining the oral history traditions of the peoples concerned as well as the written accounts of Europeans and the work of earlier ethnographers. Harris published his research in the first chapter of *The Resettlement of British Columbia*. He concluded that the pre-contact population was probably over 200,000, possibly over 400,000, and that it had been affected by "European" diseases even before direct contact with Europeans.[3] Follow Cole Harris's example and take an informed but pragmatic approach to facts. Very often, facts will be self-evident, but sometimes historians find that supposed facts rest on nothing more than assumptions and preconceptions. There are several procedures that can help in determining the truth of questionable "facts."

Check the Internal Consistency of Primary Sources

If a source contradicts itself, it is worth asking why. For example, the richest sources for rural north China in the Japanese occupation are the reports written between 1940 and 1942 by teams of sociologists who were sent by the Japanese government's South Manchurian Railway Company to interview large numbers of peasants. These reports contain many contradictions, because the peasants—for good reason—mistrusted the occupiers and sometimes lied to them. Nevertheless, historians have used the interviews as sources to reconstruct the economy, society, and politics of the region.[4] They have done so using internal inferences—in other words, by comparing discrete parts of the sources with each other. Individual peasants may have lied to the Japanese on specific issues, so all their statements must be checked against each other. The historians have then checked these sources against other sources of information on rural north China to get a better sense of which accounts are most plausible. An inconsistency in a source does not automatically taint all that source's evidence, but it should remind the researcher to probe claims carefully.

Check Primary Sources against Each Other

Comparing source materials can lead to important new inferences. One such breakthrough came when historians were examining sources for the life of Louis Pasteur, who made some of the most significant contributions to nineteenth-century biology. After Pasteur died in 1895, his colleagues and relatives published chronicles of his life that were universally admiring. Historians had some reservations about relying exclusively on such uncritical sources, but they had few alternative accounts to which they could turn. Pasteur's nephew and laboratory assistant, Adrien Loir, intimated that Pasteur had misled the judges at the public trials of the anthrax vaccine. Because Loir presented little evidence to support his claim, however, most historians continued to trust the glowing accounts of Pasteur's supporters. It was not until Pasteur's laboratory notebooks passed out of his family to the French state that historians could gain access to them. When Gerald Geison read the notebooks, he found that they confirmed Loir's account. Geison then used the notebooks to re-evaluate Pasteur's experimental practices, leading him to move Loir's account from the background to the foreground. A simple comparison of sources made it possible to make a significant inference about Pasteur, and Geison wrote an important book, *The Private Science of Louis Pasteur*.[5] Such source comparisons are at the heart of much critical thinking in history.

Compare Primary Sources
with Secondary Sources

Historical knowledge changes incrementally as new information and new interpretations alter our understanding of the past. When new materials or methods become available, historians often find themselves using primary sources to refine or contradict ideas proposed in secondary works. Sometimes the primary sources appear in surprising places—like under a parking lot. England's King Richard III was killed in battle in 1485. According to the earliest accounts, Richard's mutilated body had been buried without ceremony in an abbey church in Leicester, and the exact location was forgotten almost immediately. Following Richard's death, a rival branch of the family sat on the English throne. It was in their interests to portray Richard negatively, and when William Shakespeare wrote the play *Richard III*, he portrayed Richard as a hunchbacked, child-killing monster. Richard passed into history as a villain, and many (although not all) historians simply accepted and repeated that point of view. In 2013, archaeologists unexpectedly found a skeleton buried under what was now a parking lot. Based on its location, its age, its measurements, and the damage it showed from battle wounds, the skeleton looked consistent with historical accounts of Richard and his death. Historian and genealogist John Ashdown-Hill used his expertise to track down a Canadian descendant from Richard's family and established Richard's mitochondrial DNA sequence. This was matched with a sample from the skeleton, and yielded very convincing proof that the skeleton in the parking lot was indeed the earthly remains of England's last Plantagenet king. The discovery and identification of Richard III's body is a good illustration of how modern science can be relevant for historians. Using the primary source of Richard's body we are now able to reassess ideas about the king's health and appearance, and several historians have been inspired to re-examine the accounts of his life and his death.[6] A whole set of new directions for study has opened up and inspired historians to take another, more open-minded, look at Richard and consider to what extent he deserved his negative reputation.

Sometimes a comparison of primary and secondary sources develops insight in the other direction, because a familiar body of secondary works can help historians find a new way to understand primary sources. This happens most obviously when the secondary sources are directly relevant to the primary sources. If you are writing an essay about nutrition in seventeenth-century Quebec, for example, and using financial accounts from ecclesiastical institutions as primary sources, secondary sources on food and healthcare in New France are plainly going to be relevant. So, too, would secondary sources on these topics in seventeenth-century France and New England. You could discover, for example, that the rhubarb being purchased was not intended as a food, but rather as a medicine—the root of the plant was used as a purgative. You might also want to consult secondary sources on early modern Catholicism to help you better understand certain dietary restrictions observed in New France, such as an abstention from meat during the many fasting days of the year. You would also benefit from the insights of very different fields of study, perhaps looking to nutrition science for information on whether the foods people were eating would have provided sufficient calories and nutrients, or to geography to determine which of the foods being consumed could have been grown locally, or to anthropology to learn some theories of what makes food choices significant to a community. Secondary sources can be very helpful for historians who keep an open mind about cross-fertilization across different fields. The Parks Canada missions to find the wrecks of the nineteenth-century Franklin expedition ships HMS *Terror* and HMS *Erebus* drew upon Inuit oral history, English written history, and archaeology. The work of climate scientists has helped us better understand Norse accounts of Viking settlements in North America, the work of linguists has helped to clarify the Indigenous names of people and places in colonial archives, and the work of geneticists is helping to redraw conjectural maps of ancient human migrations.

Combine Sources to Make Inferences

During the course of your research and writing, you will be constantly reading sources in the context of other sources. You will need to check primary and secondary sources for internal consistency. You will also need to compare primary and secondary sources against each other. How might all this comparison work in practice?

Imagine you are beginning with a primary source. In this case it is the song "Cross Road Blues" by Robert Johnson, recorded in the Mississippi Delta in the 1930s. Here are the lyrics of the first verse:

> I went to the crossroad,
> Fell down on my knees.
> I went to the crossroad,
> Fell down on my knees.
> Asked the Lord above "have mercy,
> Save poor Bob, if you please."[7]

What can historians tell from only the text of this song? The singer goes to the crossroads to pray, and even as he asks God for mercy, he employs a somewhat irreverent tone. Historians know that Johnson sang it in the Delta, but the song itself does not seem to make any particular reference to the place. Standing by itself, this song may not be very interesting, at least from a historical standpoint.

Historians might be able to gain a better understanding of the song if they knew something about Robert Johnson. In a book called *Standing at the Crossroads*, historian Pete Daniel writes that as a young man Johnson knew the blues artists Son House, Willie Brown, and Charley Patton. During the 1920s, all of them worked and played in the vicinity of the Dockery plantation in the Mississippi Delta. Johnson could not play as well as the others, and at one point he simply disappeared, seemingly leaving for good. But several months later Johnson reappeared, having become a much better guitar player. The legend developed that Johnson had gone down to the crossroads and sold his soul to the Devil so he could play the blues. This legend casts some light on how Johnson's audience understood the song.[8] Historians might reasonably make the inference that Johnson played the song to perpetuate a legend among his audience.

Pete Daniel makes it possible to interpret the "Cross Road Blues" in the context of the legends surrounding Johnson's life, but it might be possible to make further inferences about the song from some other comparisons. The references to the Devil in the legend are fascinating, and perhaps another source could be found that would place Johnson's song in the context of African American religious practices. In a history of the Delta called *The Most Southern Place on Earth*, James Cobb argues that blues musicians, like other African Americans, had a different concept of the Devil from European Americans. The Devil was not a sinister Satan but a playful trickster who resembled the African god Legba. When Johnson associated himself with the Devil, he was advertising himself as dangerous, but not as European Americans might conventionally understand it.[9]

Tracing a few footnotes makes it possible to draw further inferences about African religious practices being retained in African American culture. Several essays in a collection edited by Joseph Holloway, *Africanisms in American Culture*, substantiate the case that African religious and musical practices were indeed retained and developed in African American culture. One essay by Robert Farris Thompson shows plenty of evidence to suggest that crosses and crossroads were considered to be sacred by the Kongo people, and these symbols remained important in African American art and folklore. Another essay, by Margaret Washington Creel, tells more about the significance of the cross in Kongo religious practices. Archaeological evidence and oral histories suggest that the cross was a symbol in Kongo religion long before the introduction of Christianity to the region, and that during the Christian era Kongo ideas about religion could be found in coastal Georgia and South Carolina.[10] When read in the context of this information, Robert Johnson's song becomes a significant piece of evidence for building the case that some elements of African culture survived the experience of slavery.

Creel supports her argument partly by making reference to John Janzen and Wyatt MacGaffey, who published a collection of Kongo oral histories during the 1970s. One of MacGaffey's recorded texts is particularly interesting to compare with the "Cross Road Blues." In it, a man named Kingani describes how he went to the crossroads and prayed to the spirits of his ancestors for the health of his child.[11] This Kongo text bears an obvious resemblance to Robert Johnson's song. Such a comparison does not show that Johnson was necessarily conscious of African religious traditions, but it does suggest the inference that Johnson may have been drawing on a folk tradition having its origins on the other side of the Atlantic. Making such inferences by comparisons can make it easier to appreciate any discrete piece of evidence.

Move from Inferences to Arguments

The process of making inferences allows historians to say something new. This can be an intimidating proposition, especially if you are a student working on a topic that has already been studied extensively. But judging by the contents of most bookstores, it is clear that historians are always finding something new to say about old topics. Just when you think the Roman Empire or the Second World War has been studied to death, a new book appears.

There are many ways to say something new. Sometimes, a new source appears that forces us to re-evaluate our interpretation of the past. It is more often the case, however, that new interpretations are made of old sources. Experienced historians know that new ideas come out of close and careful comparisons of primary sources and secondary sources. A new idea in one field can shed light on an old source; the discovery of a new source can inspire historians to rethink some old ideas. In fact, every individual historian brings a unique personal perspective to all sources.

Still, novelty is not enough. Small inferences must be built into larger arguments, and arguments must be made persuasively. As you read your sources, start thinking about ways to compose your essay. How can you move from asking questions about events and sources to composing a story and an argument of your own? For many scholars, this is the most challenging aspect to writing any history. You must consider the evidence of your primary and secondary sources, and then engage them constructively and responsibly to create a plausible and persuasive argument.

Make Reasonable Inferences from Your Sources

Source materials impose healthy constraints on historical writers. You may have a hunch that space aliens helped the Egyptians build the pyramids, but after careful review of primary and secondary sources you will find no good evidence to support your hypothesis. Don't worry. You thought you could make a breathtakingly new argument, but it is much more important that you recognize the limits of your sources. Do not expect too much from your sources, and do not read into them what you hope to find. If you cannot use a source to support your argument, you must be prepared either to redefine your questions or to move on to another set of sources. You might even write an essay about how little you can tell from the sources.

Make Inferences That Are Warranted

How do historians know what makes some inferences better than others?

The ancient Greeks divided arguments from inferences into two categories: **deduction** and **induction**. When you are reading and writing history, you can use these categories to help you decide which arguments from inferences are warranted.

1. **Deductive Reasoning.** In deductive reasoning, a writer makes an inference based on a limited amount of evidence, but the inference is still trustworthy because it is consonant with conventional wisdom. In other words, deduction means that we are applying general rules to particular circumstances.

Writers understand deductions by breaking deductive warrants down into their stated and unstated components. Here is an example of a historical deduction: "The gaps in the Watergate tapes must mean that Nixon was trying to hide something." What sort of evidence do historians have to support this statement? The Watergate tapes do contain large gaps, but Nixon never admitted to hiding anything; he said his secretary accidentally erased portions of the tapes. Why did most people not believe this explanation? Common sense indicates that the missing passages contained evidence that would incriminate Nixon, that he had a motive for erasing them, and that he also had the necessary access.

If you break the argument down into its deductive components, this is what it looks like:

- Evidence: The Watergate tapes contain large gaps.
- Common-sense warrant: The official explanation is less credible than the idea that the tapes were erased to destroy evidence against the president.
- Inference: When Nixon delivered the incomplete Watergate tapes to investigators, he must have been hiding something.

Although writers rarely state their reasoning in such a schematic way, common-sense deductions often provide the bases for inferences based on limited information.

It is worth remembering, though, that common sense can be deceptive. Inferences can and should be challenged by testing whether their warrants really are sound. Many people have heard the story about how Columbus wanted to prove that the earth was round. According to the legend, Columbus's contemporaries believed the earth was flat. Both this story, and people's belief in it, are based on a weak common-sense warrant:

- Evidence: The earth appears to be flat, and people in the past lacked a modern scientific understanding.
- Common-sense warrant: People can distinguish between flat objects and round objects, but nobody five centuries ago had the tools or intelligence necessary to make an accurate assessment of the shape of the earth.
- Inference: Columbus's sailors thought that the earth was flat, not round.

Obviously, people may not actually be able to distinguish flat objects from round objects, at least not on the planetary scale. But equally obviously, if you consult primary sources from medieval Europe that clearly show the earth as spherical in shape, you will see that educated Europeans at the time of Columbus knew very well that the earth was round. If your common-sense warrant does not make sense, then there must be a flaw in your reasoning. Take care to test your warrants, especially if they are unstated. If you don't test your own warrants, your audience surely will.

2.   Inductive Reasoning. Inductive reasoning is commonly associated with science, because it begins with many particular bits of evidence and generalizes from them. Induction operates on the warrant that a conclusion based on a large quantity of data is likely correct. Take this statement: "Census reports indicate that between 1890 and 1990 Canadian life spans increased significantly." What are the components of this inductive statement?

- Evidence: Census reports from 1890 to 1990 show that Canadians died at increasingly older ages.
- Inductive warrant: A large amount of data pointing to the same conclusion suggests that the conclusion is likely correct.
- Inference: On the basis of the evidence, Canadian life spans increased significantly.

The most common way to test such an inference is to question whether the evidence is sufficient to support the conclusion. The underlying inductive warrant is difficult to challenge.

Avoid Anachronisms

An **anachronism** is a chronological disarrangement, where something has been misplaced out of its proper time. When historians write history, they speak on behalf of people who lived in the past. This is a tremendous responsibility, which is why anachronistic interpretations have no place in historical writing. Although modern-day comparisons can shed valuable light on historical events, and historians can bring latter-day interpretations to bear on their subjects, you should never place your subjects in situations that they would not recognize.

Some anachronisms are easy to avoid. No sensible person would ever write this sentence: "Just before Caesar crossed the Rubicon, he glanced at his wristwatch and wondered if it would ever be time for tea." Obviously, Caesar did not have a wristwatch or tea. Other types of anachronism present subtler problems. Modern insights into political motivations, psychology, or medicine can elucidate events from the past, but historians must be careful not to presume that people hundreds of years ago thought about these things in the same ways as we do now. For example, the historian Georges Lefebvre wanted to use Marxist theory to explain the origins of the French Revolution. But when Lefebvre wrote the book *The Coming of the French Revolution*, he knew he could not argue that the French working classes intended to form a communist party and establish a dictatorship of the proletariat. Such an anachronistic claim would not have been true to the experience of eighteenth-century French people, who had never heard of such things as the communist party or the dictatorship of the proletariat. Instead, Lefebvre gained a heightened awareness of class conflict by reading Marx, and then used this awareness to ask new questions of his sources.[12] When John Mack Farragher analyzes the British expulsion of the Acadians from their colonial territories in the 1750s, he writes that this action "was the first episode of state-sponsored ethnic cleansing in North American history."[13] To make the comparison, Farragher juxtaposes the expulsion of the Acadians with twentieth-century episodes of forced migration or ethnic cleansing and demonstrates that the events in Acadia represented the latter as defined by the UN Commission of Experts in 1992. Although the term "ethnic cleansing" was unknown in the eighteenth century, Farragher establishes that the expulsion was comparable to modern events both in its purpose and in its consequences for the Acadians.

Many students become interested in history because they want to explain the origins of contemporary problems. This is a common way to ask questions about the past, but historians must also respect the outlook of people who lived in the past. For example, historians may see the origins of modern physics in Newton's *Principia*, but Newton must be understood in the context of the seventeenth century. Like many of his contemporaries, he had interests in alchemy and religion that bear little relation to modern physics and that may seem bizarre or even foolish from a modern perspective. As Betty Jo Teeter Dobbs shows in her book *The Janus Face of Genius*, it is important for a historian to understand Newton's own perspective and to ask how his understanding of mechanics related to his understanding of alchemy and religion.[14] The power of hindsight makes it perfectly legitimate to ask contemporary questions about former times, but historians must remain faithful to the perspective of the people who lived through the times under study.

Review

1. Question your sources. Consider both what the evidence does tell you, and what it does not.
2. Check facts carefully.
3. Compare evidence from a variety of sources.
4. Develop an argument based on all the evidence.
5. Be true to your characters' reality.

Notes

1. Walt Whitman, "The Real War Will Never Get in the Books," in *Specimen Days* (New York: Signet Classic, 1961), 112.
2. John H. Arnold, *History: A Very Short Introduction* (Oxford: Oxford University Press, 2000), 13.
3. Cole Harris, *The Resettlement of British Columbia: Essays on Colonialism and Geographical Change* (Vancouver: University of British Columbia Press, 1997).
4. Prasenjit Duara, *Culture, Power, and the State: Rural North China, 1900–1942* (Stanford, CA: Stanford University Press, 1988); Philip C.C. Huang, *The Peasant Economy and Social Change in North China* (Stanford, CA: Stanford University Press, 1985); Ramon Myers, *The Chinese Peasant Economy: Agricultural Development in Hopei and Shantung, 1840–1940* (Cambridge, MA: Harvard University Press, 1970).
5. Gerald L. Geison, *The Private Science of Louis Pasteur* (Princeton, NJ: Princeton University Press, 1995), 149–56.
6. John Ashdown-Hill, *The Last Days of Richard III and the Fate of his DNA* (Stroud, Gloucestershire: The History Press, 2013); Philippa Langley and Michael Jones, *The King's Grave: The Discovery of Richard III's Lost Burial Place and the Clues It Holds* (New York: St. Martin's Press, 2013).
7. Robert Johnson, "Cross Road Blues," in *The Blues: A Smithsonian Collection of Classic Blues Singers*, recorded 1936, Smithsonian Collection, 1993.
8. Pete Daniel, *Standing at the Crossroads: Southern Life in the Twentieth Century* (Baltimore: Johns Hopkins University Press, 1986; 2nd ed. 1996), 21–22.
9. James C. Cobb, *The Most Southern Place on Earth: The Mississippi Delta and the Roots of Regional Identity* (New York: Oxford University Press, 1992), 290.
10. Margaret Washington Creel, "Gullah Attitudes Toward Life and Death," and Robert Farris Thompson, "Kongo Influences on African-American Artistic Culture," in *Africanisms in American Culture*, ed. Joseph E. Holloway (Bloomington: Indiana University Press, 1990), 81–82, 154.
11. John Janzen and Wyatt MacGaffey, *An Anthology of Kongo Religion: Primary Texts from Lower Zaïre* (Lawrence: University of Kansas, 1974), 73–75.
12. Georges Lefebvre, *The Coming of the French Revolution*, trans. R.R. Palmer (Princeton, NJ: Princeton University Press, 1947; rev. ed. 1989).

13. John Mack Farragher, *A Great and Noble Scheme: The Tragic Story of the Expulsion of the French Acadians from their American Homeland* (New York: Norton, 2005), 473.

14. Betty Jo Teeter Dobbs, *The Janus Face of Genius: The Role of Alchemy in Newton's Thought* (Cambridge, UK: Cambridge University Press, 1991).

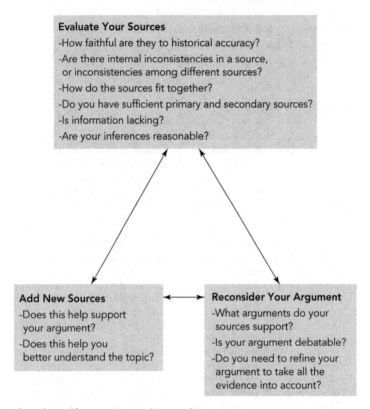

Evaluate Your Sources

-How faithful are they to historical accuracy?

-Are there internal inconsistencies in a source, or inconsistencies among different sources?

-How do the sources fit together?

-Do you have sufficient primary and secondary sources?

-Is information lacking?

-Are your inferences reasonable?

Add New Sources

-Does this help support your argument?

-Does this help you better understand the topic?

Reconsider Your Argument

-What arguments do your sources support?

-Is your argument debatable?

-Do you need to refine your argument to take all the evidence into account?

Flowchart Chapter 4   Understanding sources

5

Organizing a First Draft

After spending days, weeks, or months gathering and analyzing information, the time will come when you have to make the transition from research to writing. This transition is often the most difficult stage of a project, but it must be done. Scholars facing the empty page or blank computer screen would do well to heed the advice of Samuel Eliot Morison, one of the greatest historians of the mid-twentieth century. In an article called "History as a Literary Art: An Appeal to Young Historians," Morison advised students to avoid the temptation to find that one last source or to brew another pot of coffee. Instead of procrastinating, Morison insisted that his students should "First and foremost, *get writing!*"[1] Once you start to write, you will have to think more rigorously about what it is that you want to say. And it doesn't matter if the writing is not perfect. You will find it much easier to correct mistakes in a draft than to come up with the material in the first place.

Craft a Thesis Statement

By now, your hypothesis is beginning to take the form of a thesis statement. A thesis statement summarizes the main ideas of your argument. It guides the readers through the essay. In short **analytical essays**, it is often placed near the end of an introductory paragraph. In a longer, research-based essay, the thesis statement is often articulated after several paragraphs have introduced the underlying motive for the research by reviewing the main secondary works in the field. In either case, a basic test may be applied to see whether a thesis statement is workable. Read the statement out loud and ask yourself:

1. Is this thesis statement a claim that can actually be argued about, or would most reasonable people either simply agree or disagree with it?
2. Will it be possible to support the thesis by using recognized evidence?

If the answer to both questions is "yes," write the thesis statement at the top of a blank page. You are ready to fill the rest of the page with your **outline**.

Create a Draft Outline

By now you will also know which pieces of evidence you will be using to support your main argument. You may not yet know whether you will organize the essay as one long narrative touching on analytical topics, or as an analysis using short narratives to illustrate specific points. In the early stages of writing, it is usually a good idea to make at least one outline of your essay, and in fact you may want to make several different outlines to see which structure best suits your material. Don't worry about polishing your prose at this stage: the outlines are sketches of the broader organization of an essay to test its feasibility. A good outline gives prominence to the main argument, and it shows how any sub-arguments are related to the main argument.

Let's suppose that you have chosen to analyze the fairness and legality of Louis Riel's trial. This means that you are telling the story of the trial in order to examine an analytical problem, and your outline might look something like this:

I.   Introduction: The North-West Rebellion and its causes; the role of Louis Riel; the role of the Canadian federal government; what constitutes "fair" and "legal"

II. The trial's process
   A. Judge, lawyers, and jury
   B. Charges and main arguments
   C. Verdict and execution
III. The trial analyzed
   A. The choices of judge and jury members
   B. Riel's sanity
   C. Riel's citizenship status and the applicability of treason laws
IV. Conclusion
   A. The trial was neither entirely fair nor entirely legal
   B. Significance of this story

This essay tells a single narrative and uses it to illustrate an analytical question: the extent to which the judicial process could be subverted to the needs and priorities of the state.

Complete Analytical Outline

The draft outline above only provides a skeletal framework for an analytical essay. It may be useful as a beginning, but it doesn't do much to help you articulate your argument. To put some flesh on the bones, you need to add supporting points and details. The main point of the essay, the thesis, should be clearly stated in the introduction. The thesis statement sets up the whole paper, and everything that follows should be devoted to proving it. A complete outline of an analytical essay will show how you are moving from one analytical topic to another in order to accomplish this goal.

I. Introduction: By the early 1880s, the constituent groups in the Northwest had serious grievances against the Canadian federal government. Decision by some to ask Louis Riel to lead a protest movement. Protest erupted into armed rebellion, which was defeated. Federal government response to the rebellion and in the later judicial process was determined by federal needs rather than by the specific issues in the Northwest. This illustrates how the judicial process could be subverted by the needs of the state:

A. The government wanted to fully establish its rule in the Northwest. Suppressing and fully discrediting the rebellion helped to accomplish this goal.

B. The rebellion and trial created strong feelings amongst the populations of Ontario and Quebec, and the government had to choose whom to appease.

C. "Fairness" and "legality" have meant different things over time. This paper will use a standard widely accepted in nineteenth-century North America.

II. The trial itself is worth examining.

A. The judge and Crown (= prosecution) lawyers were easterners, chosen by the federal government.

B. Riel was charged with violating a 1352 British treason statute. Prosecution argued he was instigator and leader of rebellion, that he'd asked for a money bribe to stop the action, and that he wanted to break up Canada. Defence argued, over LR's objections, that he was insane and therefore not criminally responsible.

C. Judge instructed jury on definition of insanity and reminded them about the bribe. Jury deliberated quickly, verdict of guilty but with plea for mercy in sentencing. Judge said death.

III. Analysis of trial suggests several issues of fairness and legality.

A. Judge was a federal political appointee, not in a permanent position, so was anxious to please Ottawa. Disliked Métis and spoke no French. Judge sided with Crown to ensure trial in Regina rather than BC or Ontario as defence asked; this ensured the 6-man, Anglophone, Protestant jury, rather than 12—less chance of hung jury with 6. All lawyers easterners.

B. Riel does seem to have been behaving strangely (explain this) and had spent time in an American asylum. His lawyers thus argued for his insanity— but he was adamant he was sane. Big argument between him and his lawyers meant his defence was not whole-hearted or coherent.

C. Riel had formally and legally renounced his loyalty to the Queen and taken on American citizenship years earlier—was 1352 treason law applicable? They could have gone with Canadian treason statutes of 1862 or 1866, but those did not carry death sentence.

IV. Conclusion: Louis Riel was executed, and this is not a surprise in the circumstances.

A. The outcome of the trial was predetermined both by the Canadian federal government's determination to extend full control over the West and by their decision to appease the Anglophone, Protestant population of Ontario. The process was fundamentally flawed in several respects of fairness and legality. The fact that they chose the 1352 statute suggests a desired conclusion.

B. All of the above demonstrates and foreshadows a larger and longer set of struggles, which still continue to the present: federal–provincial, Anglophone–Francophone, and White–First Nation and Métis.

This detailed outline is organized around analytical points, with evidence presented in short narrative accounts.

Draft Outline of a Narrative Essay

It's also possible to organize an essay around a single chronological narrative, in this case an account of the 1885 North-West Rebellion that focuses on Riel's involvement and includes important analytical points. Here is a simple draft outline of that **narrative essay**:

I.   The South Saskatchewan in 1885
    A.   General description
    B.   The stakeholders and their specific grievances
II. Riel returned from the USA
    A.   How and why he came back
    B.   Riel's actions as leader
III. The events of the rebellion
    A.   Duck Lake, Fish Creek, Batoche
    B.   The rebellion ends
IV. The aftermath
    A.   Trials, imprisonment, and executions
    B.   The effects of rebellion

Complete Narrative Outline

A complete outline of a narrative essay on the rebellion and Riel would include brief references to analytical issues:

I.   The South Saskatchewan:
    A.   The area was rural, old HBC trading territory; had been buffalo country, but buffalo now disappearing. This threatened especially the livelihoods of the Métis. Poor harvests in the early 1880s threatened everybody. The territory in the charge of the federal government now, but the government generally not following through on its responsibilities.
    B.   Short discussion of Saskatchewan society, including Métis, First Nations, and White settlers. Discussion of their various grievances, including government reluctance to guarantee Métis title to their own lands and farms, attempts to force First Nations onto reserves, failure to grant much in the way of local government powers, decision to move planned CPR line further south. The federal government's actions and

inactions were largely responsible for the rebellion (an analytical point).

II. Riel returned.

    A. He was invited back in 1884 by a delegation of Métis. (Note that these represented a small group of the most militant; most Métis would not be involved in the rebellion.) He was well educated locally and in Quebec, multi-lingual, and charismatic. Métis himself, his leadership of the resistance to the federal government in 1869–70 had led to the creation of Manitoba as a province, so he was a natural choice even though he'd been in the USA for years (an analytical point).

    B. Riel helped in fall of 1884 to create a petition to the federal government—no result. Also instrumental in creating Métis "Bill of Revolutionary Rights" in spring 1885. Comment on the contents of this declaration (analytical point) and on his efforts to get peaceful resolution of the Métis grievances. March 1885, the Métis create provisional government with Riel as president. Analysis of this group and of their immediate actions re: Batoche and HBC Fort Carlton demonstrate increasing militancy.

III. The events of the rebellion.

    A. Describe briefly and discuss the military events. Duck Lake (March 26), negotiations with North-West Mounted Police floundered and shots were fired. Dead and wounded on both sides, but police essentially lost. Riel saved them from pursuit. Feds send in troops and militia, using CPR line—eventually about 5000 of them. First Nations now gearing up for real war. Fish Creek (April 24), FN won—again no pursuit. Batoche (May 9–12), hard fought, but Métis lost.

    B. Riel surrendered May 15—analyze why he didn't just flee to USA. Some First Nations kept going, but big defeat in late May led to surrenders; final surrenders in early July.

IV. The aftermath.
   A. Discuss briefly the charges against and trials of the various participants, and speculate on why the Crown used different charges, and even different treason statutes, against them. Concentrate on trial of Riel and of the First Nations' leaders. Briefly outline the sentences.
   B. Comment on the effects of the rebellion, which were felt by all parties in the Northwest but also resonated hugely in Ontario and Quebec. Discuss the results also in Ottawa. End with mention of Riel and the North-West Rebellion now, and the way in which all of this has helped to shape Canada.

This detailed outline shows how a straightforward chronological narrative can incorporate important analytical content.

The essay outline is a step on the way to a final product (the essay itself). Unless you are asked to follow a specific form, you have a lot of options for how the outline should look. Some people like the flexibility of using index cards, where they write one main idea on each card, and move these cards around on a table until they have found the smoothest path to proving a thesis. Others prefer mind maps for the space they give writers to link ideas together in multiple ways. Choose whatever form is most likely to help you find the best structure for your essay.

Start to Write a First Draft

The complete outlines given above are built on frameworks for sustained arguments. It is not enough that a historical essay have an introduction, a series of paragraphs with evidence, and a conclusion; a good historical essay leads its readers in some direction. It can be challenging for a writer to articulate and sustain this direction, which is one of the reasons why an argument can be helpful. An argument is not an angry display of vituperation; it is an idea that develops over the course of an essay. It should capture and hold an audience's attention, and it must be proven using evidence and reason.

As you think about how to turn your outline into a first draft, go back to your notes to find support for your possible arguments, and compose paragraphs around them. It is fine to start with paragraphs that will fall in the middle of the essay if this seems best. An introduction does not have to be written first. Indeed, you may wish to write this part of the essay later. As you grapple with writing about your sources, you will discover new things about them, things that will make an early version of the introduction obsolete by the time you finish the body of the text.

While you are writing the first draft, keep your argument in mind and think about how it is evolving. As you add more analysis and information, stand back occasionally to check and see whether your overall argument is developing in a reasonable and interesting way. You may find yourself changing your line of argument to the point where it does not resemble your original argument any more. If this happens, return to the beginning and check the entire argument for consistency.

Catch Your Reader's Attention, but Do It Gently

Every reader asks, "Why should I read this?" A writer must give the reader a reason to care. Many historians use the beginning of an essay or book to connect their scholarly interests to broader academic and political debates. For example, in a book called *Holy Feast and Holy Fast*, which is about medieval religious women in Western Europe, Caroline Walker Bynum begins with a quick discussion of the scholarship in her field. Then she grabs the reader's attention:

> Sex and money ... again and again modern scholars have emphasized the guilt engendered by their seductiveness, the awesome heroism required for their renunciation. Yet this modern focus may tell us more about the twentieth century

than about the late Middle Ages. In our industrialized corner of the globe, where food supplies do not fail, we scarcely notice grain or milk, ever-present supports of life, and yearn rather after money or sexual favors as signs of power and of success.[2]

Notice the tone of Bynum's paragraph. It addresses topics of universal interest like sex, money, and food, but it does so calmly and methodically. You do not need to drop a bomb to get your reader's attention. Be relevant, but use a light touch. People prefer to read essays they find agreeable, trustworthy, and authoritative. Even when you suspect your audience may disagree with you, it behooves you to treat them with some moderation. Put them in the right frame of mind to listen to your argument.

Another strategy for catching the reader's attention is to open with an event or idea from the history you are presenting. This may take the form of a quotation from a primary source, or an account in your own words of an important moment. Allan Greer begins his book *Mohawk Saint: Catherine Tekakwitha and the Jesuits* with an engaging description of the scene at a crucial moment in his historical subjects' lives:

> He came to visit her every day, as she lay waiting to die.
>
>   It was the spring of 1680, during the Catholic season of Lent, and Catherine was scarcely able to rise from her mat on the floor of the bark-covered longhouse. Much of the time she was alone with her illness, lying close to a smoldering fire; at her side were a carved wooden dish with her day's supply of corn porridge and some water in a bark bowl. Only a handful of women, children, and old people remained in this Christian Iroquois village on the banks of the St. Lawrence, and during the day they were busy outdoors gathering firewood or preparing the ground for spring planting. Most of the men and many of the women were still many days' journey to the north or the west, at their hunting camps along the Ottawa and its tributaries. They would return for Easter, laden with beaver skins and other furs to discharge their debts with the French merchants

of Montreal. Then there would be solemn church services and jubilant feasting, but now Kahnawake (or Sault St. Louis, as the French called it) was generally quiet.[3]

By beginning Chapter 1 this way, Greer is able to introduce some of the main people and places in his book while giving his readers a vivid sense of Catherine Tekakwitha's world, both material and spiritual. An advantage to this kind of opening is that it draws your reader immediately into the centre of your paper's topic. If you can include a direct quotation from a primary source, or if you are able to portray the world of your historical subjects with sufficient sensitivity to their reality, your introduction's flavour of authenticity will invite the reader to set aside preconceived notions and read your paper with an open mind.

State Your Intellectual Interests Early

In an academic paper, your readers will also expect you to give them a sense of your intellectual interests. What broader historical problems does your essay address? Why have you chosen this specific topic to explore these problems? What argument will you be developing over the course of the essay? Address these questions at or near the beginning of your essay, or else you will run the risk of confusing and losing your readers.

For an example of how these questions can be answered effectively in an introduction, consider the beginning of an article by Samuel K. Cohn, Jr about the Black Death:

> HIV/AIDS and the threat of biological warfare have refueled interest in the Black Death among professional historians, biologists, and the public, not only for assessing the toxic effects of the bacillus but for understanding the psychological and longer-term cultural consequences of mass death. This article makes two arguments. Against the assumptions of historians and scientists for over a century and what continues to be inscribed in medical and history texts alike, the Black Death was

not the same disease as that rat-based bubonic plague whose agent (*Yersinia pestis*) was first cultured at Hong Kong in 1894. The two diseases were radically different in their signs, symptoms, and epidemiologies. The proof of these differences forms the major thrust of this article. The second argument stems from the epidemiological differences between the two diseases. Humans have no natural immunity to modern bubonic plague, whereas populations of Western Europe adapted rapidly to the pathogen of the Black Death for at least the first hundred years. The success of their immune systems conditioned a cultural response that departs from the common wisdom about "plagues and peoples." As far back as Thucydides, historians have seen the aftershocks of pestilence as raising the level of violence, tearing asunder secular cultures, and spawning pessimism and transcendental religiosities. A fresh reading of the late medieval sources across intellectual strata from merchant chronicles to the plague tracts of university-trained doctors shows another trajectory, an about-face in the reactions to the plague after its initial onslaught. This change in spirit casts new light on the Renaissance, helping to explain why a new emphasis on "fame and glory" should have arisen in the wake of the West's most monumental mortality.[4]

In this introduction, Cohn captures the reader's interest by mentioning present-day fears of epidemic diseases and biological weapons. Then he quickly introduces two related arguments that will interest anyone who has ever read about the Black Death. The first is that the Black Death may not have been caused by exactly the same disease as people had for a long time assumed. The second argument, growing from the first, is that Europeans appear to have gradually developed immunity to the pathogen that caused Black Death, and this immunological success may have inspired people, rather than disheartening them.

Cohn's arguments are radical. He presents them as "paradigm shifts" that overturn more than a century of scholarship on the Black Death. Cohn highlights the originality of his argument, yet he establishes a reasoned tone that will cause even the most skeptical historians to consider his arguments carefully. He does not write scathingly about previous historians. Instead, he uses an excellent strategy. He starts to build his case in the first paragraph by giving us a glimpse of the evidence he has considered: "late medieval sources" ranging from "merchant chronicles to the plague tracts of university-trained doctors."

When an audience begins to read Cohn's article, they know why they should be interested; they know which problems the author is addressing; and they have some idea of how the author will approach these problems. In his first paragraph, the author has given his readers much to anticipate.

The example from Cohn's article shows how an argument—in more than one part—may be made in the opening of an essay. Usually historians state this argument clearly and concisely near the opening of the essay in what is called the "thesis statement." Some professors prefer for students to conclude the introductory paragraph with a clear argument, while others allow for some flexibility. Either way, place a clear thesis statement near the beginning of the essay, so that readers may grasp your argument as early as possible.

Historian Paul Josephson begins his essay "The Ocean's Hot Dog: The Development of the Fish Stick," with a clear thesis statement (italicized here to make it easier to see):

> The fish stick—the bane of schoolchildren who generally consider it an overcooked, bread-encrusted, cardboard-tasting, fish-less effort of lunchrooms and mothers to deceive them into consuming protein—is a postwar invention that came into existence as the confluence of several forces of modernity. These forces included a boom in housing construction that contained kitchens with such new appliances as freezers, the seeming appeal of space-age ready-to-eat foods, the rise of consumer culture, and an increasingly affluent society. *Yet the fish stick arose during the 1950s not because consumers cried out for it and certainly not because school children demanded it but*

because of the need to process and sell tons of fish that were harvested from the ocean, filleted, and frozen in huge, solid blocks. Consumers were not attracted by the form of these frozen fillets, however, and demand for fish products remained low. Manufacturers believed that the fish stick—a breaded, precooked food—would solve the problem. Still, several simultaneous technological advances had to take place before the product could appear.[5]

The first sentence catches our attention and then situates the seemingly banal fish stick in a serious discussion. The thesis statement tells us that the developers of the fish stick did not sense a strong demand; on the contrary, they had an oversupply of frozen fish and needed to get rid of it! The wider significance of this argument is that supply, rather than demand, can drive the history of innovation.

Review the Historical Literature

All historians know that reading deeply and widely helps us become better analysts. In their writing, therefore, they build common ground with their readers and their colleagues by demonstrating knowledge of their topic's historical context, and they situate themselves within the historical discussion. Historians' essays often include a review of the scholarship in one or more fields of history. In an essay entitled "Putting the Ocean in Atlantic History," Jeffrey Bolster begins by writing that most historians of the Atlantic world have overlooked the history of the ocean itself. To demonstrate that he knows Atlantic history well enough to make such a claim, he summarizes the field in general terms, writing that it is "known for blurring historiographical and disciplinary boundaries, ignoring national boundaries, and probing novel social and cultural interactions," adding a footnote that references a dozen key recent works. He compares Atlantic history to the history of other oceanic regions, stating that "proliferating histories of oceans and seas are reorienting conventional geographies and emphasizing oceans as access points for innovative regional histories." Another footnote references another dozen sources. Bolster then reviews those historians who have written about the political and economic history of the Atlantic, with a footnote to half a dozen sources. Bolster praises historians, journalists, and ecologists who are working together to understand changes to marine ecologies, with eight references to their work. He concludes that most historians slight the role of nature in the modern Atlantic world, and then he cites the work of seven historians who do successfully incorporate nature. Further references are made to environmental historians who do or do not engage with the history of the oceans. This scholar leaves no doubt in anybody's mind that he has done the kind of background reading that is essential to his ultimate argument: that between 1500 and 1800 New Englanders transformed the Northwest Atlantic, which in turn transformed their own societies.[6] Student writers need not demonstrate their mastery of such a vast body of scholarship that would develop over the course of thirty years. Even so, remember that knowledgeable readers will want any writer to demonstrate familiarity with recognized, authoritative writing about their subject area. Such familiarity indicates to readers that the author will make trustworthy observations.

Build Your Essay with Good Paragraphs

A paragraph is much more than just an indented block of text. Good paragraphs develop inferences from sources, and they also contribute to the overall argument of the essay. To accomplish all this, here is what the best paragraphs do.

1. **Make a Transition from the Previous Paragraph.** Readers want to know why they are moving from one paragraph to the next. Good paragraphs connect to each other with one or two **transition sentences**, signposts that remind readers where they have been and tell them where they are going.

2. State the Point of the Paragraph. Each paragraph presents and develops a point that supports the overall argument of the essay. Sometimes the point may be located in the transition or "signpost" sentences; other times you may wish to write a separate "thesis sentence."

3. Present Evidence to Support the Point of the Paragraph. What sort of evidence do you have to support the point of this paragraph? Present the information from your sources that has helped you make historical inferences, and explain why the evidence presented here advances the argument.

In the abstract, these three components of the paragraph sound easy to manage. In reality, it takes discipline and creativity to put this advice into practice. The best historical writers produce paragraphs that blend together a transition, an argument, and evidence, but there are many ways to do this. No one common structure will work for every paragraph.

If you are looking for a model of successful paragraphing, consider Daniel Headrick's history of the global spread of European technologies, *The Tools of Empire*. In the fourth chapter, Headrick discusses how firearms changed during the nineteenth century:

> At the beginning of the nineteenth century the standard weapon of the European infantryman was the muzzle-loading smooth-bore musket. It had a flintlock to detonate the powder through a hole in the breech and a bayonet that could be attached to the barrel for hand-to-hand combat. The Brown Bess, which British soldiers used until 1853, was much the same weapon their fore-fathers had carried at Blenheim in 1704. It had an official range of 200 yards but an effective one of 80, less than that of a good bow. Despite admonitions to withhold their fire until they saw the whites of their enemies' eyes, soldiers commonly shot away their weight in lead for every man they killed. These muskets took at least a minute to load, so to maintain a steady rate of fire on the battlefield, soldiers were drilled in the countermarch, each rank advancing in turn to shoot, then falling back to reload.

One of the most serious drawbacks of the flintlock muskets was their poor firing record. Under the best conditions, they fired only seven out of ten times, and in rain or damp weather they ceased firing altogether. For this reason soldiers were trained to use their weapons as pikes. In 1807, Alexander Forsyth, a Scottish clergyman and amateur chemist, offered a solution to this problem; using the violent explosive potassium chlorate as a detonating powder and a percussion lock instead of a flintlock, he made a gun that could fire in any weather. Tests showed that a percussion lock musket misfired only 4.5 times per thousand rounds, compared to 411 times for a flintlock. After 1814, Joshua Shaw of Philadelphia improved upon Forsyth's invention by putting the detonating powder into little metal caps, thereby simplifying the loading process and making the weapons even more impervious to the elements.[7]

Notice how Headrick makes the transition from the first to the second paragraph. In the first paragraph, he was discussing some of the drawbacks to the old muzzle-loading muskets. He begins the second paragraph by telling readers that he is now going to discuss one of the most *serious* problems. Readers are still learning from him about problems with muskets, but he is introducing them to a new way of evaluating the weapons. Headrick also presents plenty of evidence (and in the original text, each paragraph ends with a note to his sources). The paragraphs develop ideas; they are supported by evidence; and they relate closely to the broader argument the author is making about the history of firearms. Headrick's paragraphs guide readers by relating the significance of the evidence to his broader point.

Define Your Key Terms Early

Do not assume that you and your audience understand important concepts to mean the same thing. Define key terms as soon as you introduce them. You will find that you can use a definition as a springboard to discuss the complexities of your subject.

1. **Defining Uncommon Terms.** Sometimes you will need to define specialized or foreign terms that your audience might not recognize. In an article called "Plunder or Harmony? On Merging European and Native Views of Early Contact," Toby Morantz discusses a common First Nations' distinction between *atiukan* and *tipachiman* accounts of their own history. Knowing that most of her readers will not be familiar with these words, Morantz explains that while the *atiukan* part of the oral tradition "refers to myths, stories concerning the creation of the world when people and animals were not differentiated," the *tipachiman* accounts "are about real people—living, or their ancestors—but not necessarily without reference to what western thinking would label the supernatural."[8] Morantz's definition is clear, but she also implicitly suggests that the First Nations' perspectives of reality are not exactly the same as those from other backgrounds. Thus Morantz uses her definition to invite her readers to consider the larger issue of competing views and interpretations of reality, which is a central part of her argument.

2. **Redefining Common Terms.** In addition to defining unfamiliar terms, sometimes you will need to redefine commonly used English words. This is exactly what William Cronon does in his book *Changes in the Land.* The *Canadian Oxford Dictionary* defines "landscape" as "natural or imaginary scenery as seen in a broad view," but Cronon uses the word more broadly. When he looks at the ecological transformation of colonial New England, he tells a story that relates the management of natural resources to cultural and political debates among the Indigenous Americans and English settlers. Cronon's New Englanders saw that the "landscape was a visible confirmation of the state of human society."[9] An English landscape, a way of viewing and ordering the world, prevailed over an Indigenous American landscape. You will sometimes also need to redefine geographic terms. If you are writing about the early colonial history of "Canada," do you mean the area of European settlements along the St Lawrence River

that the French called "Canada" in the seventeenth century, or the area within the boundaries of the state called "Canada" today?

Set an Appropriate Tone

All historians must build a relationship with their audience. The best way to establish rapport is to find an appropriate, trustworthy tone.

1. Be Judicious and Dispassionate. All historians pass judgment on their subjects, but don't be too heavy-handed. If your subjects engaged in some particularly horrible activity, it is important to strike a balance between the rendering of judgment and the presentation of evidence. Some of the most difficult evidence to handle comes from Nazi Germany, and here are two historians who built trustworthy arguments by using a judicious, dispassionate tone.

Psychiatrist and historian Robert Jay Lifton wanted to learn why medical doctors served the Nazi regime. He uses Dr Josef Mengele as a case in point—a horrifying case indeed. Lifton writes in his book *The Nazi Doctors* that Mengele "committed real crimes, murderous crimes, direct murder. . . . These crimes included selections, lethal injections, shootings, beatings, and other forms of deliberate killing." All this is well known, but the power of Lifton's work comes from his dispassionate argumentation. He describes Mengele's "research" matter-of-factly and puts Mengele's experiments in the context of the Nazi's medical career: "More than any other SS doctor, Mengele realized himself in Auschwitz. There he came into his own—found expression for his talents." Mengele remained the consummate clinical researcher, even in the midst of a concentration camp. Lifton presents Mengele objectively and ironically, so that readers will trust the book's conclusion: that Mengele had a schizoid personality, making it easier for him to detach himself from the suffering he inflicted on others.[10]

It is often enough just to describe a horrible activity in a clear and direct way. Your readers will recognize through your description that you find this activity repugnant. William Sheridan Allen wanted to learn how the Nazis came to power. Instead of focusing on well-known politicians in Berlin, he wrote a book called *The Nazi Seizure of Power* that focuses on the activities of the Nazi Party (NSDAP) in a small German town called Northeim. He describes how the Nazis used public events to sustain enthusiasm for their cause:

> Then on Sunday, March 19, the Northeim NSDAP gave its victory celebration, fittingly held in the Cattle Auction Hall. The hall, decorated with swastika flags, was full to the bursting point with at least a thousand people. The chief speaker was the Nazi preacher, Pastor Muenchmeyer, and his topic: "What a Transposition Through Divine Disposition!" The whole tone of the celebration was conservative, solemn, and religious.[11]

Allen does not call the Nazis cattle; the Cattle Auction Hall is an appropriate place for their meeting. He does not say that the pastor and his audience are intellectual mediocrities; he gives the title of the speech. Allen makes his point—that the Nazis were dangerous, obsequious drones—cleverly and subtly in a reasoned tone.

2. Keep the Focus on the Writing, Not the Writer. Generally speaking, you should be directing your readers to think about the history rather than the person who presents it. For some students, this means avoiding the first-person pronoun altogether. Instead of writing "I will argue," for instance, they write "this paper will show." While you may decide to take the same approach, and in fact you may be directed by your instructor not to use the first person singular, many historians do speak about themselves and their ideas using the first person. They may introduce their own interpretation with "my research suggests," or begin a summary of their impression with "it seems to me." There is no need to shun a simple and straightforward phrase like "I think" if it saves you from the more convoluted "it can be thought that," but you may want to read carefully through any sentence where you have written a first person pronoun to see whether it can be removed without changing the meaning. Instead of writing "Therefore, I conclude that the outcome of Louis Riel's trial was predetermined both by the Canadian federal government's determination to extend full control over the West and by their decision to appease the Anglophone, Protestant population of Ontario," write instead "The outcome of the trial was predetermined both by the Canadian federal government's determination to extend full control over the West and by their decision to appease the Anglophone, Protestant population of Ontario." That this is your conclusion should be obvious from the context: its placement in your essay, and the well-reasoned argument leading up to it. Stay away from the phrases "in my opinion" and "I believe" entirely: your analysis should be based on evidence and reason, not opinion and belief.

One case where historians often employ the first person singular is when they have personally experienced a phenomenon they are describing and want to introduce this personal information to explain their own relationship to the subject matter. For example, Carl Degler begins his book about racial thinking in anthropology, *In Search of Human Nature*, by writing, "Like most white Americans of my sex and class (the son of a fireman) and my generation (born in 1921) I came into a world that soon made me a racist and a sexist."[12] He does this to draw the reader's attention to personal and social issues of bias. He also honestly informs readers that he bears a close personal relationship to his subject, something they may wish to know when they evaluate his arguments.

Treat Other Writers with Consideration

Scholarship can be a very fragile enterprise. It thrives on lively debate and open disagreement, but it depends on mutual respect and careful consideration. When you write about other historians, give them the same amount of respect you would give if you were speaking to them in person. Never oversimplify or misconstrue the arguments of other writers, and do not make personal attacks on opponents to discredit their arguments. You don't have to agree with what other writers have said, but you must be polite and fair in your discussion of their work.

Account for Counterarguments

Do not select just one argument and ignore all the other possibilities. When you acknowledge the possibility of alternative interpretations you increase the credibility and complexity of your own work. Your readers will not think you are weak; they will think you are open-minded and well-informed. In fact, your readers may already be aware of some possible contradictions to your argument, and they will expect you to deal with them.

By the very nature of their work, historians know it is impossible to write a flawless interpretation of anything. In a short essay, it is often effective to note a few main counterarguments toward the end, and then conclude by reasserting why you still wish to articulate your own position. In a longer essay, thesis, or book, authors often engage in multiple counterarguments as they consider the evidence.

One such example of counterargumentation can be found in Robert McElvaine's book *Eve's Seed: Biology, the Sexes, and the Course of History*. McElvaine reviews evidence from prehistory and also from evolutionary psychology that suggests humans are adaptable social animals who are both competitive and cooperative. Their cooperative side inclines them to build families and groups in which both sexes work together. For most of human history, differences between the sexes did not necessarily result in the subordination of one sex to another. McElvaine argues it was the Agricultural Revolution, starting around 10,000 BCE, that caused men to subordinate women. According to McElvaine, men lost their roles as hunters, and then, out of insecurity and envy, they turned to misogyny. Patriarchy in the home mirrored male domination in politics, religion, and business. Male domination is not natural or inevitable; it can be explained historically.

To make this argument, McElvaine has to address two possible counterarguments: first, that human behaviour is completely determined by biology, and second, the opposite argument, that all people are born with a clean slate and it is nurture, not nature, that is important.

McElvaine wants to show that nature and nurture are both important. First, he engages these two opposite positions with a joke. Quoting his own father in an early chapter title, he writes that people are "90 percent nature and 90 percent nurture." Next he moves to consider the "nurture" position. McElvaine writes:

> The reason that so many liberals have clung to their insistence that human nature should be ignored is, I believe, a fundamental misapprehension concerning the implications of human nature. They have feared that the admission of the existence of innate characteristics will lead to findings on how people differ. In fact, the real meaning of human nature, as [Franz] Boas understood, is to be found in showing the ways in which people are alike. As Robert Wright has said, unlike the old social Darwinists, "today's Darwinian anthropologists, in scanning the world's peoples, focus less on surface differences among cultures than on deep unities."

After considering the "liberal" position, McElvaine turns to the "conservatives," who often believe in the determining power of genetics over human nature. He quotes from the work of Richard Dawkins and Edward Wilson, two sociobiologists who have written that people "are machines created by our genes," and that "human behavior . . . is the circuitous technique by which human genetic material has been and will be kept intact. Morality has no other demonstrable ultimate function." In response to these "biodeterministic" arguments, McElvaine writes:

> As Darwinism had been a century and more ago, sociobiology has been latched onto by people who seek to justify the unjustifiable. Conservatives seize on the principle of natural

selection to maintain that everything that exists should be left alone, because it was made that way by the god of adaptation. But this is not so. It ignores genetic drift, whereby characteristics come into being that provide no evolutionary advantage, but also no disadvantage, and so survive despite Darwinian selection, not because of it. The actual essence of the Darwinian principle of selection is not that a trait must be well adapted in order to survive, but that it not be poorly adapted relative to other traits. It is possible for some features to continue to develop after they have fulfilled their original evolutionary function. Human intellectual ability is probably an example of this. It grew far beyond what was necessary for human survival in the eons during which it was physically developing (although perhaps not beyond or even up to what is necessary for survival in the nuclear age; indeed it may yet prove to be ultimately maladaptive by destroying the species).

McElvaine's summary of the conservative and liberal positions on human nature is balanced and fair-minded, even though he strongly disagrees with these views. By reporting and engaging opposing arguments, McElvaine makes it more likely that liberals and conservatives will treat his argument with serious consideration.[13]

Lead Your Readers to an Interesting Conclusion

Over the course of your essay, you will propose a thesis, then offer evidence, analysis, and inferences as you develop your main argument. By the time you reach your concluding paragraph, your readers will be ready for you to put your ideas back into a broader context.

There is no formula for a concluding paragraph, just as there is no formula for an introductory or supporting paragraph. Even so, there are certain things historians look for in a conclusion. A conclusion should reflect on the essay and answer the "Who cares?" question once again. A strong conclusion will not simply repeat the introduction. If the essay has truly sustained and developed an idea, then there should be a new way to sum things up. How are the findings of the essay significant? How might the findings of the essay change how the readers think?

One example of an interesting conclusion can be found in Mercedes Steedman's article "The Red Petticoat Brigade," about RCMP surveillance of the Ladies' Auxiliary of the Mine, Mill, and Smelter Workers Union of Sudbury, Ontario, during the Cold War era. Why would the RCMP have spent decades monitoring an organization devoted as much to bake sales as to labour activism? Steedman concludes that the surveillance reflected contemporary fear of the perceived threats posed by communism, as well as post-war concern over the proper place of women in society:

> The RCMP surveillance of innocuous social groups was part of a larger social construction of Cold War culture, one that turned neighbour against neighbour and generated a general climate of suspicion. In this way RCMP surveillance served to constrain the character of working-class post-war activism for both men and women. For working-class women activists, these constraints of post-war "normalcy" meant that women who openly advocated women's equality and social justice were immediately suspect, even when they were holding tea parties. Yet Mine Mill women did actively promote a greater voice for women of the day. Through the auxiliary movement, working-class women worked for the cessation of weapons testing, for full disarmament, and for the creation of conditions that, as Dorothy McDonald reported, "would enable women to fulfill their roles in society, as mothers, workers, and citizens which includes the right to work, the protection of motherhood, equal rights with regards to marriage, children and property."[14]

Steedman summarizes her argument and then goes beyond it to suggest that the Mine Mill women were in fact early activists in what would later become known as the women's liberation movement. She reminds her readers of the significance of what they have been reading, and she even leaves the last word to her historical subject.

When you are writing a conclusion to your essay, provide your readers with a reminder of the main findings of your research and a suggestion for how to appreciate the significance of your argument. Then end with something both memorable for the reader and appropriate to the subject matter.

Review

1. Explain your purpose and methods clearly.
2. Structure your argument carefully.
3. Define your terms.
4. Deal with counterarguments.
5. Write an engaging and meaningful introduction and conclusion.

Notes

1. Samuel Eliot Morison, "History as a Literary Art: An Appeal to Young Historians," *Old South Leaflets* 2, no. 1 (Boston: Old South Association, 1946): 7.

2. Caroline Walker Bynum, *Holy Feast and Holy Fast: The Religious Significance of Food to Medieval Women* (Berkeley and Los Angeles: University of California Press, 1987), 1.

3. Allan Greer, *Mohawk Saint: Catherine Tekakwitha and the Jesuits* (New York: Oxford University Press, 2005), 3.

4. Samuel K. Cohn, Jr, "The Black Death: End of a Paradigm," *American Historical Review* 107, no. 3 (June 2002): 703. Cohn's citations have not been included in this quotation.

5. Paul Josephson, "The Ocean's Hot Dog: The Development of the Fish Stick," *Technology and Culture* 49, no. 1 (January 2008): 41. Emphasis added.

6. W. Jeffrey Bolster, "Putting the Ocean in Atlantic History: Maritime Communities and Marine Ecology in the Northwest Atlantic, 1500–1800," *American Historical Review* 113, no. 1 (February 2008): 19–47, references to pp. 19–23.

7. Daniel Headrick, *The Tools of Empire: Technology and European Imperialism in the Nineteenth Century* (Oxford, UK: Oxford University Press, 1981), 85–86.

8. Toby Morantz, "Plunder or Harmony? On Merging European and Native Views of Early Contact," in Germain Warkentin and Carolyn Podruchny, eds., *Decentring the Renaissance: Canada and Europe in Multidisciplinary Perspective* (Toronto: University of Toronto Press, 2001), 53.

9. William Cronon, *Changes in the Land: Indians, Colonists, and the*

Ecology of New England (New York: Hill and Wang, 1983), 6.

10. Robert Jay Lifton, *The Nazi Doctors: Killing and the Psychology of Genocide* (New York: Basic Books, 1986), 341, 378.

11. William Sheridan Allen, *The Nazi Seizure of Power: The Experience of a Single German Town, 1922-1945* (New York: Franklin Watts, 1965; rev. ed. 1984), 207.

12. Carl Degler, *In Search of Human Nature: The Decline and Revival of Darwinism in American Social Thought* (Oxford, UK: Oxford University Press, 1991), vii.

13. Robert S. McElvaine, *Eve's Seed: Biology, the Sexes, and the Course of History* (New York: McGraw-Hill, 2001), 26-32.

14. Mercedes Steedman, "The Red Petticoat Brigade: Mine Mill Women's Auxiliaries and the 'Threat from Within,' 1940s-70s," in *Canadian Working-Class History: Selected Readings*, ed. Laura Sefton MacDowell and Ian Radforth, 3rd ed. (Toronto: Canadian Scholars' Press, 2006), 327.

Write an Introduction (although you don't have to write this first)	- Grab the reader's attention gently - Demonstrate the significance of the topic - State the thesis and describe how the paper will prove it
Organize Ideas Logically and Meaningfully	- Decide which framework (narrative, analytical) better suits the argument - Arrange points sensibly - Provide evidence to support each point, and analysis to show the reader how it is linked to the thesis - Anticipate and account for counter-arguments
Link Ideas, Sentences, Paragraphs	- Provide transitions so that the reader can follow your thoughts - Ensure that each paragraph is linked to the thesis - Balance quotes and summaries with analysis
Think about Language and Tone/Consider Your Audience	- Define terms as necessary - Keep the tone judicious and dispassionate - Focus your reader's attention on the writing, not the writer
Conclusion	- Remind the readers of the thesis - Offer a new perspective on the significance of the research

Flowchart Chapter 5   Writing your first draft

6

Structuring Your Paper with Good Narrative Techniques

You may decide to organize your essay into one long narrative, or you may choose to organize it along analytical lines by using short narratives to illustrate particular points of analysis. In either case, narrative structure is central to the writing of history.

Build a Narrative That Tells a Story

Narratives tend to share some easily recognized components: a narrator, an organization, a setting, and one or more characters. Not all history is written in the same narrative form as a novel or an epic poem, but many good examples of historical writing are shaped as an overarching narrative supported by shorter narratives and well-chosen details. A story within a story often illustrates the general argument. During the fifth century BCE, a Greek adventurer and storyteller named Herodotus wrote one of the first historical narratives. He used dramatic tension and colourful description to help his readers imagine the past. While recreating the Persian invasion of Greece in 480 BCE, Herodotus described how the Persian emperor Xerxes and his huge army destroyed the small contingent of Spartans guarding the pass at Thermopylae. Herodotus did not simply say that the outnumbered Spartans were brave and fought to the death, nor did he just tell his audience that the Spartans were calm when the massive Persian forces came into sight; he described how the Spartans ignored the Persians and combed their hair. Instead of enumerating every episode of bravery, Herodotus selected the story of one Spartan soldier named Dieneces for special mention:

> It is said before the battle he was told by a native of Trachis that, when the Persians shot their arrows, there were so many of them that they hid the sun. Dieneces, however, quite unmoved by the thought of the strength of the Persian army, merely remarked: "This is pleasant news . . . if the Persians hide the sun, we shall have our battle in the shade."[1]

Herodotus' mastery of narrative helped make his stories—and his vision of history—so enduring.

Write a Narrative to Support an Argument

Herodotus was not just telling a story about a gutsy warrior at Thermopylae. He was selecting specific events to illustrate a broader interpretation. Historians use such anecdotes and stories in support of their arguments, and the best storytellers can wrap a powerful argument within a seamless narrative. When Herodotus presented his work to the Athenian public, he used dramatic techniques to make a connection with his audience: Xerxes lost the war because he had too much pride, the downfall of many a character in Greek drama. Herodotus told the story of Thermopylae because he wanted to show in a colourful way that the Spartans had fought bravely in defence of a united Greece. He also wanted to draw a stark contrast between the Greeks, who died willingly for their liberty, and the Persians, whose leaders had to whip their troops to make them fight.[2] In the story as Herodotus tells it, the Greeks were clearly superior. Herodotus, like other historians, used a narrative to make an argument, and that argument was supported by specific evidence.

Combine Chronology with Causation

In narratives, historians use time to give structure to the past. For this reason, most narratives have some chronological features: a beginning, a middle, and an end. This may seem simple, but in the hands of a skilled historian a narrative's events do not just follow each other; early events cause subsequent events to happen.

If you are crafting a narrative, your first task will be to select influential events and then place them in a sensible chronological order. This is vital to understanding the causes of things, and it is not as easy as you may think. For example, historians draw on the accounts of both Muslims and Christians when they write about the Crusades. The two religions kept different calendars, however, meaning that historians must translate the dates of one into the dates of the other to form a coherent chronology. Sometimes you will not know a firm date for an event; you must do your best to place it in relation to another source. Fifteenth-century parish records from Scotland tell when children were baptized, but not always when they were born. If you wish to establish an individual's date of birth, you will have to find another source that tells you how long families waited before having their children baptized. Another thing to remember when assembling your chronology is that there is not necessarily a causal relationship between events that follow one another: event B can follow event A without having been caused by event A. It rained this morning after I put my umbrella away, but my decision about the umbrella did not cause the precipitation. The Titanic struck an iceberg on 14 April 1912 after its passengers ate a lavish supper, its orchestra played fashionable music, and one of its lookouts cried, "Iceberg, right ahead!" None of these things, however, caused the collision. The logical fallacy of assuming that an event was necessarily caused by an earlier event is called the *post hoc ergo propter hoc* logical fallacy, meaning "after this therefore because of this." Determining whether two successive events have a causal relationship or not can prove to be among the most complex, and the most interesting, of historical questions. Norse settlements on Greenland collapsed not long after a cooling of the climate in the fourteenth century. The colder temperatures made seas rougher, which in turn made travel to Europe and to the walrus hunting grounds more dangerous, and the cold and wind made it increasingly difficult for the Norse to continue their traditional systems of agriculture and pastoralism. In spite of these challenges the Norse adapted successfully for multiple generations before they disappeared. Climate change was almost certainly a contributing factor to the collapse of the Greenland Norse settlements, but scholars continue to debate to what extent, and in what ways, it might have constituted a cause.

Get a Sense of Change and Continuity

Placing events in a chronology is more than just an exercise. It helps you understand change over time, which is an abiding interest among historians. Once you have established the sequence of events, you will begin to get a sense of how some things changed over time while other things remained the same. In 1833, the British Parliament emancipated all colonial slaves. For more than thirty years politicians and activists had been debating abolishing the slave trade, ameliorating the lives of enslaved people, and emancipating them from bondage. From the perspective of a Barbadian, slave emancipation may have come as a sudden and dramatic change in status. But that interpretation could be too simple. After emancipation, former masters invented numerous ways to coerce former slaves. Sugar production still required land, labour, and capital, all of which remained available to plantation owners and unavailable to former slaves. It is debatable whether former slaves felt more continuity than change.[3] As this example shows, human societies are sufficiently complex that not all their members experienced change in the same way, and not all changes brought about the intended consequences.

Select the Key Participants in Your Story

If you were telling a narrative of emancipation in Barbados, you might choose to focus on former slaves and masters. You might also work on enslaved women entrepreneurs, previously freed townsmen, colonial bankers, or government officials. Remember, your story must make an argument. Do certain individuals illustrate the argument of your narrative better than others? Were certain individuals more significant agents of change than others? Do you have access to more detailed evidence about some people than others? You may wish to exclude some people from your narrative altogether, or relegate them to the background. Justify your choice, and limit your use of extrapolation accordingly.

Find Your Voice as a Narrator

Discovering your own voice as a narrator will be especially challenging in your early efforts at writing academic history. Every historian does this differently, but one rule always applies: every narrator must be as faithful as possible to the people and events of the past.

1. The Omniscient Narrator. Some historians prefer to recede into the background, telling their story from the perspective of an omniscient outsider while refraining from making comments about themselves or their engagement with the source materials. In his account of India's anticolonial rebellion of 1857, *The Great Mutiny*, Christopher Hibbert uses this style of narration. He is arguing that the rebellion began when British officers ordered Indian troops (*sepoys*) to use a new kind of bullet cartridge:

> One day in January 1857 a low-caste labourer at Dum-Dum asked a sepoy for a drink of water from his *lota*. The sepoy, being a Brahmin, had naturally refused: his caste would not allow him to grant such a request; he had just scoured his *lota*; the man would defile it by his touch. "You will soon lose your caste altogether," the labourer told him. "For the Europeans are going to make you bite cartridges soaked in cow and pork fat. And then where will your caste be?"[4]

2. The Uncertain Narrator. Not all historians feel that their sources permit such an omniscient narration. In fact, great controversy surrounds the origins of this 1857 rebellion. Sometimes historians use a less certain tone in narration to reveal the ambiguities of their source materials. Writers can even strengthen a narrative by informing readers of the limits in their interpretations. John Demos uses such a strategy in a book called *The Unredeemed Captive*, which is about Eunice Williams, an English girl who was captured by Mohawks in the Deerfield Massacre of 1704. After her abduction, Eunice adapted to the ways of the Kahnawake Iroquois. This disturbed her family, but it did not stop them from trying to bring her back to Massachusetts. Demos worked with limited sources, mostly the letters and diaries of Eunice's English relatives. The family spent decades trying to learn about Eunice, but in the end they recorded very little information. Demos struggled to extract meaning from these scarce sources, but his narrative is at its most compelling when he speculates about the changes in Eunice's life:

> Different it was, very different. And yet, within a relatively short time, it took. By 1707, Eunice was reported to be "unwilling to return." And the Indians—including, one would presume, her new family—"would as soon part with their hearts" as with this successfully "planted" child.[5]

Demos makes it clear in his writing, with phrases like "was reported to be" and "one would presume," that he is not claiming to know the full truth about what happened. If you know that you do not know something for certain, let this knowledge inflect your narrative voice: be clear about what is unclear, and confident about your lack of confidence.

Choose Your Beginning and End

The past is interconnected across chronological and geographical boundaries, but every narrative must have a beginning and an end. You will find it challenging to decide when to start and stop your story. Hibbert begins his story of the 1857 rebellion with a description of a typical working day for Sir Thomas Metcalfe, British representative to the king of Delhi.

> He returned from his office at half past two for dinner at three. After dinner he sat reading for a time before going down to the billiard-room. A game of billiards was followed by two hours spent on the terrace contemplating the river. Then it was time for a light supper and an evening hookah. Immediately the clock struck eight, he stood up and went to bed, undoing his neckcloth and throwing it, together with his well-tailored coat, on to the floor to be picked up by the appropriate servant. If this or any other servant did not perform his duties to the master's entire satisfaction, Sir Thomas would send for a pair of white kid gloves which were presented to him on a silver salver. These he would draw on with becoming dignity, then firmly pinch the culprit's ear.[6]

Hibbert is not just telling a story about an indolent, auto-cratic colonial official. He uses the beginning to set the scene for a larger story about how Indians rebelled against British author-ity, how British forces crushed the rebels after great loss of life, and how this experience transformed South Asia and the British Empire.

Hibbert sets the opening scene in Delhi because his narrative will reach its climax when the British recapture the city. His nar-rative ends when the British banish the king of Delhi:

> The trial lasted more than two months; but the verdict was never in doubt. On 29 March he was found guilty on all charges and later sentenced to be transported for life to Rangoon. He left Delhi in October accompanied by Jawan Bakht, another young son whom he had had by a concubine, and by a most-unwilling Zinat Mahal who, by now "quite tired of him," de-scribed him as "troublesome, nasty, cross old fellow." He died

on 7 November 1862 in Rangoon where the descendants of his son, Jawan Bakht, are still living today.[7]

Hibbert concludes his narrative at this point for a number of reasons. The rebellion ended in different ways for different people, but for Hibbert it is the exile of the king of Delhi that represents the end of the rebellion. One of the causes of the rebellion had been a dispute over who would succeed the king. Much of the rebellion had taken place in and around Delhi. The exile of the king draws several strands of the story to a close, while Hibbert mentions the descendants of the king as a way of emphasizing the enduring legacy of the rebellion. Follow Hibbert's example when you conclude a historical narrative: choose a beginning and an ending that suit your story and your argument.

Supply a Meaningful Title

The title is the first thing a reader sees from your paper, so make sure it will leave a good impression. Don't waste the opportunity to introduce readers to your essay by leading with something as uninspiringly generic as "Assignment #1" or "History Research Essay." Don't diminish the seriousness of your work with too flashy a title either. Puns, clichés, and double entendres can strike a sour note and might alienate your audience. A good title should convey some idea of what the paper is going to be about, set the right tone, and fit easily onto one or two lines.

Review

1. Use well-chosen anecdotes to make deliberate points.
2. Consider causes and consequences, continuities and changes.
3. Control your materials by picking the characters and events you need to make your argument.

Notes

1. *Herodotus, The Histories,* trans. Aubrey de Sélincourt (New York: Penguin Classics, 1954; rev. ed. 1983), 519.

2. Chester W. Starr, *A History of the Ancient World,* 4th ed. (New York: Oxford University Press, 1991), 294–95.

3. Franklin W. Knight, *The Caribbean: The Genesis of a Fragmented Nationalism,* 2nd ed. (New York: Oxford University Press, 1990).

4. Christopher Hibbert, *The Great Mutiny: India 1857* (New York: Penguin Books, 1978), 63.

5. John Demos, *The Unredeemed Captive: A Family Story from Early America* (New York: Vintage Books, 1994), 146.

6. Hibbert, *Great Mutiny,* 24.

7. Hibbert, *Great Mutiny,* 388.

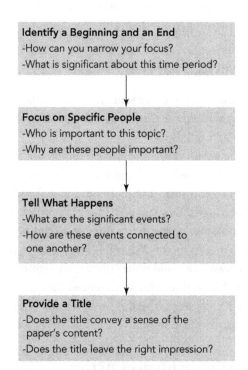

Identify a Beginning and an End
-How can you narrow your focus?
-What is significant about this time period?

Focus on Specific People
-Who is important to this topic?
-Why are these people important?

Tell What Happens
-What are the significant events?
-How are these events connected to one another?

Provide a Title
-Does the title convey a sense of the paper's content?
-Does the title leave the right impression?

Flowchart Chapter 6 Representing the past

7

Writing Sentences

Historians share a common goal with all writers: to communicate ideas effectively.[1] They differ from other writers, however, on some of the conventions for achieving this goal. The differences can be confusing for students trained in other disciplines, but no historical convention is arbitrary; they all help historians represent the past as accurately as possible. Follow these conventions to make your writing lively, clear, and persuasive.

Choose Verbs That Are Precise

Verbs form the heart of every sentence because they convey the action. To craft sentences that are direct and clear, select precise verbs and avoid vague ones.

What is a vague verb? The most common are forms of the verb "to be"—"is," "are," "was," and so on. These words are indispensable, but their overuse can make writing dull and lifeless. It's true that "the Mughal Emperor Akbar was in power for forty-nine years," but you would make the point more vigorously by writing that "the Mughal Emperor Akbar reigned for forty-nine years." In the same way, you could write "there were eighteen leaders at the meeting," but "eighteen leaders attended the meeting" sounds better. If you find yourself writing with a verb of being, try to think of a more precise alternative.

Make Passive Sentences Active

One of the purposes of historical writing is to uncover who did what, as well as when, how, and why they did it. The **passive voice** often obscures exactly the kind of information the historian is trying to uncover. Indeed, the passive voice can obliterate historical actors altogether: "New France was surrendered in September 1760." By whom? To whom? If you can't state with certainty that "Governor Vaudreuil surrendered New France to General Amherst in September 1760," then you may well be confused. At the very least, you owe your readers an explanation. Even if you include all the same information about the historical actors, a sentence with verbs in the passive voice reads as cumbersome and unclear. "After China was invaded by the Mongols, the Yuan dynasty was founded by Kublai Khan" is not as quick and easy to understand as "After the Mongols invaded China, Kublai Khan founded the Yuan dynasty." The **active voice** is usually preferable when referring to historians' work too. "It is argued by Singh that the soil was exhausted by land being overly farmed" is much less clear than "Singh argues that overfarming exhausted the soil." As you read more history, you may notice that the passive voice is often a sign of weak reasoning, insufficient information, or a lack of confidence. This is not necessarily true of other disciplines. Some authors, especially natural scientists, use the passive voice to downplay their personal involvement in research. In fact, one of the biggest challenges for historians of science is to cut through this prose and learn just how scientists did involve themselves in research.

There are circumstances when the passive voice is a good fit for historical writing. It works well if you wish to emphasize the thing being acted upon rather than the people doing the acting. "Blue and white porcelain was manufactured in China, but its characteristics were designed to suit Middle Eastern tastes" puts the focus on the porcelain, whereas "the Chinese manufactured blue and white porcelain, but they designed its characteristics to suit Middle Eastern tastes" draws more attention to the Chinese who were making it. A passive verb can also be used to draw attention to a historical actor if placed near the end of a sentence. "The queen sang the most beautiful song in the concert" is a perfectly fine sentence, but if it's the queen's performance that you want to emphasize, you might want to write instead that "the most beautiful song in the concert was sung by the queen." Even though there are some circumstances when passive verbs are appropriate, when used too often they can confuse the order of ideas and make your writing seem timid. Use them sparingly.

Write (Mostly) in the Past Tense

Historians write almost everything in the past tense. This is not an arbitrary peculiarity. If you are discussing events that took place in the past, it makes sense to use the past tense. The historians' preference for the past tense can, however, be somewhat confusing for students more accustomed to writing about literature, because scholars of literature tend to write about authors and their works in the present tense. A scholar who writes about Susanna Moodie's *Roughing It in the Bush*, first published in 1852, as a literary text, uses the present tense to say that

> in Canada, Moodie is no longer a child but a mother, and her experience of loss is no longer that of the orphan but of the bereaved mother. As she "bears the word" here, the figure of her other country is both sustained and literalized, and both the mother country and Moodie the mother become associated with those experiences most resistant to symbolic representation, life and death.[2]

A scholar using Moodie's *Roughing It in the Bush* as a source for the history of nineteenth-century Upper Canada uses the past tense to say that

> on one occasion Susanna Moodie found herself face to face with the frightening unpredictability of a clearing fire that had run wild near her house, with "red forks of lurid flame as high as the tree tops, igniting the branches of a group of tall pines that had been left standing for saw-logs."[3]

Both scholars are writing about the same text, but the one who is treating it as a piece of literature speaks about it in the present tense, whereas the one who is using it as a historical source uses the past tense. Literary classics have a powerful effect on readers today, but historians want to place Moodie's writing within the context of her life and times. They discuss her observations in the past tense because she was writing in the nineteenth century.

When historians want to write about events that took place at different times in the past, they can make use of the past perfect tense, also called the pluperfect tense. This tense indicates that an action happened before another action in the past. It is formed by placing the auxiliary verb "had" before the past participle of the main verb: "Before signing the treaty, he had considered all the options." "When she arrived at school, she began to doubt what her father had always told her about ghosts." The past perfect tense has been receding for some time from both spoken and written English, and many people would consider it perfectly correct to use the simple past in its place. Often, this will have little or no effect on the clarity of the sentence. Sometimes, however, employment of the past perfect can help the reader get a more precise sense of the sequence of events. Consider this passage: "The queen needed a better sense of the enemy's strengths and weaknesses. Her brother fought in their ranks, so she sent her spies to ask him." The writer has left the precise sequence of events ambiguous. Was the queen's brother fighting in the ranks of the enemy at the same time as she needed a better sense of their strengths and weaknesses, or before? If the former, you would improve the clarity by writing it like this: "The queen needed a better sense of the enemy's strengths and weaknesses. Her brother was fighting in their ranks at the time, so she sent her spies to ask him." If the brother was no longer fighting in the ranks of the enemy, you would make the sequence clearer with this: "The queen needed a better sense of the enemy's strengths and weaknesses. Her brother had fought in their ranks, so she sent her spies to ask him."

The one circumstance in which historians do regularly use the present tense is when they are discussing recent scholarship or living scholars. They could write that "*The Return of Martin Guerre* is a brilliant examination of identity and everyday life in early modern France, which it presents through a captivating tale of imposture," and that "in *Paris 1919: Six Months That Changed the World*, Margaret MacMillan shows how the doomed efforts of the negotiators haunt us still."

Put Your Thoughts in an Intelligible Order

When arranging words and clauses into a sentence, put them in an order that your readers will quickly understand. This is not as easy as it sounds. After weeks of reading about a historical topic, you will be steeped in the complexities of how people, ideas, and events are interrelated. But when you write, you must unravel that complexity and place your ideas in a sequence that will make sense to those who have not been immersed in the research.

1.   **Keep Related Words Together.** You may think it makes sense to say "The tail-gunner saw a cloud form over Hiroshima in the shape of a mushroom," because you already know how these ideas are related. Nevertheless, your audience can only get a sense of the relationship of ideas from the way you place the words, and in this case the words are placed in such a way to suggest that the city of Hiroshima was mushroom-shaped. The audience would understand the sentence better if you wrote, "The tail-gunner saw a mushroom-shaped cloud form over Hiroshima." If you keep related words together, you will lead readers seamlessly through your sentence rather than forcing them to pause at the end to sort out the jumble.

2.   **Keep Subjects Close to Verbs.** The principal relationship in a sentence is between the subject and the verb. Do not put too much between them. Generally speaking, it is acceptable to insert a short statement between a subject and verb, as in "Eleanor Roosevelt, the

First Lady, wrote a syndicated column." But too much between the subject and the verb disrupts the flow of ideas. Take a look at this sentence: "Eleanor Roosevelt, during the presidency of Franklin Roosevelt, wrote a syndicated column." To read this sentence, you must hold "Eleanor Roosevelt" in the back of your mind until you find out what she is doing. The sentence would flow more smoothly if it were rewritten like this: "During the presidency of Franklin Roosevelt, Eleanor Roosevelt wrote a syndicated column."

3.   Make Sure That Pronoun References Are Clear. A pronoun substitutes for a noun. As the writer, you understand which noun a pronoun replaces, but your readers must infer the relationship from the way you place the words. Unless you have avoided all ambiguity, that can be difficult. Consider this sentence: "John A. Macdonald's 1864 partnership with George Brown demonstrated his political practicality and flexibility." Does "his" refer to Macdonald or to Brown? A reader might infer that, since "his" is closer to "Brown," the practicality and flexibility are Brown's. But this may not be your meaning. Both Brown and Macdonald were talented politicians, and both could be described as practical and flexible. There are several ways of recasting the sentence to avoid such confusion: "John A. Macdonald demonstrated political practicality and flexibility in his 1864 partnership with George Brown," or "John A. Macdonald's 1864 partnership with George Brown demonstrated his own political practicality and flexibility," or even "John A. Macdonald's 1864 partnership with George Brown demonstrated Macdonald's political practicality and flexibility." In each case, a minor adjustment will create a much clearer sentence.

Begin a Sentence on Common Ground and Gradually Build a New Point

Writing a sentence is not just about arranging words in an orderly way. A sentence is a place to establish or develop an idea, and a well-written sentence gives the reader a sense of direction. In other words, a sentence does not function in isolation: it needs to connect in some way with sentences on either side of it. Consider this sequence of sentences about the spice trade in late medieval Europe:

> On the eve of the Portuguese discovery of the sea route to India, in November 1496, four galleys arrived from Alexandria in Venice with at least 2 million kilograms of spices, of which 1,363,934 were pepper and 288,524 kilograms were ginger. The quantities of spices imported into Europe were impressive. In the late fifteenth century Venice acquired 412 tons of pepper from Alexandria and another 104 tons from Beirut in an average year. For specific years, some estimates surpass even these amounts. In 1496, four ships came from Alexandria to Venice with over a million kilograms of spices. Half of this was pepper.

Here the reader has to jump from a specific statement about amounts of pepper and ginger to a general statement about the size of the spice trade and then back to another specific statement. A better sequence would move from the general to the specific, as Paul Freedman does in his article "Spices and Late-Medieval European Ideas of Scarcity and Value":

> The quantities of spices imported into Europe were impressive. In the late fifteenth century Venice acquired in an average year 412 tons of pepper from Alexandria and another 104 tons from Beirut. Some estimates for specific years surpass even those amounts. In November 1496, one the eve of the Portuguese discovery of the sea route to India, four galleys arrived in Venice from Alexandria with at least 2 million kilograms of spices, of which 1,363,934 were pepper and 288,524 ginger. In the same year another convoy of four ships came from Alexandria with over a million kilograms of spices, of which half was pepper.[4]

In this sequence, sentences are smoothly connected to one another, and the reader understands from the general statement at the start what is significant about the subsequent details.

Place the Emphasis at the End

If you are developing your ideas over the course of a sentence, then the end of the sentence should be interesting and emphatic. The different arrangements in the following examples affect what the reader is likely to weigh as most significant:

1. Although food supplies were running short, he decided that they must push on.
2. He decided that they must push on, although food supplies were running short.

In the first example, the decision to continue is likely to strike the reader as the more significant point. In the second, it is the trouble with the food supplies that seems more significant. The same effect can be produced by ending a list with what you want your readers to remember as important. In the following examples, rice wine receives more emphasis in sentence number 2 than in sentence number 1, and more emphasis still in sentence number 3:

1. At the court of the Emperor, they sought rice wine, silk kimonos, and Buddhist scrolls.
2. At the court of the Emperor, they sought silk kimonos, Buddhist scrolls, and rice wine.
3. They sought silk kimonos and Buddhist scrolls at the court of the Emperor, but also rice wine.

Construct Parallel Forms

Parallel construction is a kind of repetition in which related ideas are expressed in a rigorously similar grammatical form. For example, on 8 October 1940, as Nazi bombers were pounding Britain, Churchill told the House of Commons that "Death and sorrow will be the companions of our journey; hardship our garment; constancy and valour our only shield. We must be united, we must be undaunted, we must be inflexible."[5] He constructed the first sentence loosely around the repetition of "our," but he constructed the second sentence tightly around the repetition of "we must be." Parallel construction helps the reader see similarities in content and form, and can impart a sense of relentlessness in an elegant fashion.

Vary the Form and Length of Sentences

A variety of sentence types will help relieve the monotony of bland writing. Make some short and punchy. With others, loosen the structure so that your readers—attentive as they may be—can relax for a moment and glide more smoothly through your paragraphs.

In your endeavour to write different kinds of sentences, do make sure that you are avoiding incomplete and run-on sentences. In principle, a sentence can truly be a sentence only if it has both a subject and a verb; if it lacks either of these things, it is incomplete. Generally speaking, incomplete sentences do not fit easily into formal writing. Except sometimes for interjections. Interjections like this last phrase add punch and colour, but are most effective when used rarely.

Run-on sentences and comma splices should also be avoided. A run-on sentence occurs when two complete sentences are joined without any punctuation: "The Haitian Revolution was inspired in some ways by the French Revolution it also took a more radical turn." A comma splice occurs when two complete sentences are joined without the placement of an appropriate conjunction: "The Haitian Revolution was inspired in some ways by the French Revolution, it also took a more radical turn." There are several ways to fix these errors. The most simple is to use a period: "The Haitian Revolution was inspired in some ways by the French Revolution. It also took a more radical turn." Another solution is to use a coordinating conjunction such as "but," "and," "or," "nor," "for," "so," or "yet": "The Haitian Revolution was inspired in some ways by the French Revolution, but it also took a more radical turn." Alternatively, you can use a subordinating conjunction such as "although," "because," "if," "since," "unless," "whether," "before," or "once": "Although the Haitian Revolution was inspired in some ways by the French Revolution, it also took a more radical turn." One of the most elegant solutions, if done correctly, is to use a semicolon: "The Haitian Revolution was inspired in some ways by the French Revolution; it also took a more radical turn."

There are two main ways to use the semicolon in your writing. The first is to join two closely related independent clauses into one sentence: "Marco Polo was certainly an excellent traveller; Rabban Bar Sauma, though less well known today, was easily his equal." The semicolon here indicates that the two sentences, although independent grammatically, are connected at the level of content. The second use of the semicolon is to separate elements in a long and complex list, especially if those elements contain internal commas: "Travel to distant lands in the fourteenth century required physical stamina to endure hardships of weather and terrain, not to mention the plague spreading through Eurasia; mental perseverance to think through the various stages of crossing whether by land or by sea; and, perhaps most importantly, good shoes." In this case, the semicolon helps guide the reader to know where one item on the list ends and the next begins.

Break the Rules If You Must

Guidelines are helpful, but there are times when too strict an observance of them will force you to write unnatural or ugly sentences. Good writers know when to stray from conventions and break rules to good effect. Your first task is to get your meaning across, and to do so persuasively.

Review

1. Make every sentence count.
2. Pay special attention to verbs.
3. Use word order to your advantage.

Notes

1. Much of the advice in this chapter is drawn from the classic book *The Elements of Style*, also known by its authors' names of Strunk and White. Many editions have been published. Among the most charming is William Strunk, Jr., and E.B. White, *The Elements of Style*, illustrated by Maira Kalman (New York: The Penguin Press, 2005).

2. Bina Freiwald, "'The Tongue of Woman': The Language of the Self in Moodie's *Roughing It in the Bush*," in *Re(dis)covering our Foremothers: Nineteenth-Century Canadian Women Writers*, edited and with an introduction by Lorraine McMullen (Ottawa: University of Ottawa Press, 1990), 166.

3. J. David Wood, *Making Ontario: Agricultural Colonization and Landscape Re-Creation Before the Railway* (Montreal: McGill-Queen's University Press, 2000), 141.

4. Paul Freedman, "Spices and Late-Medieval European Ideas of Scarcity and Value," *Speculum* 80, no. 4 (2005): 1214–15.

5. John Bartlett, *Familiar Quotations: A Collection of Passages, Phrases, and Proverbs Traced to Their Sources in Ancient and Modern Literature*, 16th ed. (Boston, London: Little, Brown & Co., 1992), 620.

8

Choosing Precise Words

Word choice can make all the difference to a historian, so choose your words precisely. The past abounds with catastrophic examples of poorly chosen words. One such example is the 1840 Treaty of Waitangi, in which the British took New Zealand from the Maoris by mistranslating the word for "sovereignty."[1] This deliberate act of imprecision has caused a century and a half of injustice and bad feelings.

Because words matter, get into the habit of checking your essays for word choice, which is also known as diction.

Be Concise

Some people believe they can demonstrate the complexity of their thoughts by writing sentences that are bursting with unnecessary words. They are wrong. You will give readers the clearest possible picture of your ideas if you make every word count. Why write "It is an undeniable fact that William the Conqueror was very instrumental in establishing the Norman regime" when you might easily say "William the Conqueror established the Norman regime"? If you can say something in seven words, why say it in sixteen? Being concise does not mean that all your sentences should be short and choppy; it means that you should not try your readers' patience.

Write in Language That Your Audience Can Easily Understand

Most historians write in language that non-specialist readers can understand. This tendency sets history apart from some other disciplines, whose practitioners may use a lot of **jargon**, a specialized language that helps people within the field communicate but tends to shut everyone else out. Sometimes historians will borrow jargon from other fields. For example, the *Canadian Oxford Dictionary* defines "hegemony" as "leadership or dominance, esp. by one state or social group over others," but for professional historians the word is associated with the theoretical writings of an Italian philosopher named Antonio Gramsci, who used it in the sense of social power or dominance. If you are writing for historians, you can probably expect them to understand the term as you do, but to a wider audience "hegemony" may seem to be incomprehensible jargon. The same could be said for terms associated with literary criticism and social sciences that mean different things in different disciplines, such as "Other," "subjectivity," and "narrative." When in doubt, use ordinary language or define your terms. Otherwise, an overuse of jargon can make it look like you are either trying to make yourself seem important or avoid precise commitments. In his famous essay "Politics and the English Language," George Orwell imagined how a bureaucrat might translate a passage from the King James Version of the Bible (Ecclesiastes 9:11):

> I returned and saw under the sun, that the race is not to the swift, nor the battle to the strong, neither yet bread to the wise, nor yet riches to men of understanding, nor yet favour to men of skill; but time and chance happeneth to them all.

Here is Orwell's translation into the obscure, pompous language of government:

> Objective consideration of contemporary phenomena compels the conclusion that success or failure in competitive activities exhibits no tendency to be commensurate with innate capacity, but that a considerable element of the unpredictable must invariably be taken into account.[2]

Orwell's point is clear: the overwrought language of jargon writers is no match for the simple words, natural rhythms, and clear imagery of the original passage.

Avoid Both Pretentious and Colloquial Language

Don't rely on big, complicated words to make your writing look educated or formal. You risk confusing your readers and sounding pretentious. If you say that central planning had a "procrustean" effect on Soviet engineering, for example, you might alienate your audience in two ways. If your readers do not know that the word means a ruthless disregard for special circumstances, your argument will lose its force. If they know what it means but think it seems out of place, your writing will sound inflated as though trying to compensate for some deeper weakness.

Note that most history instructors expect that you will write in formal English. Formal here does not mean stuffy or boring, but it does mean that you should avoid slang, contractions, and an overly casual tone. Such informal language, also known as **colloquial language**, may be inserted as part of a quotation, and you may also use colloquial language outside of formal, academic writing. (This book, for example, has a less formal tone than most works of history.) Unless instructed otherwise, your history essays should be written in a formal tone.

Part of this formal tone is the way historians refer to people, whether other historians or historical subjects, in their writing. The first time you introduce a person, use their full name. "Henry Louis Gates Jr presents his readers with a refreshing perspective on African-American history." "Marguerite Bourgeoys crossed the Atlantic seven times." "Joan of Arc's childhood was typical in many respects." In subsequent references, use the person's last name unless there is another part of the person's full name that is the more formal to use. "Gates writes persuasively," "Bourgeoys watched carefully," "Joan finally accepted."

Avoid Euphemisms

Do not confuse sensitivity with **euphemism**, a mild or vague word intended to replace something thought to be too harsh or blunt. Recent history seems to have been especially rich in euphemisms: torched villages were "pacified," totalitarian regimes were "people's republics," and used cars were "pre-owned vehicles." Say what you really mean, and be direct. Write that a historical figure was pregnant when she died, not that she was "with child" when she "passed."

Choose Figurative Language Carefully

When historians write about subjects that are unfamiliar to their readers, it often helps to make an imaginative comparison with something the readers likely know already. These comparisons sometimes take the form of metaphors and similes. It would be perfectly acceptable to write that "Mahatma Gandhi took part in the decolonization movement of India." It might be better to use a slightly more informative metaphor: "Mahatma Gandhi played a leading role in the decolonization movement of India." Some might think it even more effective to say that "Mahatma Gandhi was the Nelson Mandela of India," although you would probably have to sustain the metaphor by specifying the respects in which they resembled one another. Metaphors and similes add colour to historical writing, but it takes practice to use them well.

There are several ways for a metaphor to go awry. Suppose, for instance, that you had described Gandhi as "the Nicolás Bravo of India." For one thing, chances are that most people reading an essay on Indian history would never have heard of Bravo, a conservative politician who led a rebellion against the president of Mexico in 1827–8. But the comparison is hopelessly flawed in any case because Bravo's armed revolution failed while Gandhi's political one succeeded. Metaphors and similes can add vitality to your writing, but only if they make sense to your readers and remain true to historical realities.

Eschew Clichés

Readers generally welcome colourful language, but they will find your colours boring if they are entirely predictable. Colourful expressions that have been overused are called **clichés**.

Use this simple test to spot a cliché. You are using a cliché if you can remove the last word from the phrase and your readers can automatically fill it in:

- "Queen Elizabeth knew that all that glitters is not . . . (gold)."
- "The situation looked bad, but every cloud has a silver . . . (lining)."
- "The bubonic plague reared its ugly . . . (head)."

Replace clichés with plain language or less predictable metaphors.

Don't Use Unfamiliar Foreign Words

Historians often use foreign words or expressions in their writing. Some foreign terms have come into common English usage, as in "Nehru was a politician *par excellence*," or "The right of *habeas corpus* is fundamental to Canadian law."

The basic rule of thumb is to use terms that your audience understands. Imagine that you are writing about the history of the AmaXhosa, a group of people who live in South Africa. If you were taking a seminar on southern African history, and you were writing for an instructor who was a specialist in the field, it might be appropriate for you to spell out the name "AmaXhosa." This is because specialists in southern African history know that this group of people forms the plural of their collective name by adding the prefix "ama." If you were writing for a more general audience—say, in a survey of world history—you might use the more familiar English term and call your subjects "the Xhosa." It is important to know your audience's capabilities and to meet them on common ground.

Be Aware of Changes to Usage

Historical writing has always reflected the politics of its times. Today historians are demonstrating their awareness of discrimination by avoiding intolerant or biased language. Most historians recognize that all traditions are invented, including linguistic traditions, and they also recognize that people ought to be allowed to come up with a name for themselves. Thus "Negro" and "coloured" changed to "black," and then "black" started to become "African-American" and "African-Canadian," and now in some cases a preference is emerging again for "Black" or "black" as adjectives, as in "Black Canadian" and "black residents of the city."

In Canada, "Indian" as a word for an Indigenous person has largely been replaced by other descriptors. While "Native" is still quite widely used in the United States, it holds negative connotations for many in Canada. As a general rule, when referring to a specific group, use the name of that group as the group self-identifies, such as "Anishinabeg" and "Tsleil-Waututh." For larger groups, choose other appropriate descriptors. "First Nations" is a term used by many, although not by all, reserve-based communities. The "Métis" are an Indigenous group comprised of various communities whose members are descendants of unions between Indigenous peoples and Europeans. In the singular, a person from a Métis group is also "Métis." The "Inuit" are another Indigenous group, historically resident in the Arctic. "Inuit" is plural; the singular form is "Inuk." Thus "The Inuk woman who told the story," but "the group of Inuit confronted Frobisher's men." Neither Métis nor Inuit are First Nations. When referring collectively to First Nations, Inuit, and Métis people, current usage favours "Aboriginal" and "Indigenous." Note that both words should be used as adjectives rather than nouns, and that the initial letter should be capitalized when referring to people, as with other demographic groups ("South Americans," "English," etc.).

Problems can arise when quoting from earlier texts, whether primary sources or older secondary sources, which employ terminology that is now out of date. One option is to retain the terminology of your sources and supply preferred terms for modern readers. Another is to replace words from the sources with preferred alternatives. Susan Hill's first endnote in *The Clay We Are Made Of: Haudenosaunee Land Tenure on the Grand River* explains that "Unless otherwise noted, Haudenosaunee terminology will be given in the Kanyen'keha (Mohawk) language."[3] You can explain what the source means and what you mean, as Micah A. Pawling does: "The Indigenous people of the St John River Valley refer to themselves as the *Wəlastəkwewiyik, Wəlastəkwiyik, Wəlastəkokewiyik,* and *Wəlastəkokewinowək.* The different spelling systems in Maliseet and Passamaquoddy expand the four names to eight. Since there has been no agreement yet on which one to use in English, I defer to Maliseet scholar Andrea Bear Nicholas and use the affiliation 'Maliseet' or 'Maliseets' (personal communication with Andrea Bear Nicholas, April 2016)."[4]

Gender inclusivity is another area where expectations have shifted. In 1891, Oscar Wilde wrote, "Anybody can make history. Only a great man can write it."[5] His point was to draw a distinction between historical actors and the people who write about them, as well as to call attention to the challenge of writing history well. It's possible that when Wilde wrote this statement, he had no intention of ruling out the possibility of great women historians, but people today are likely to be distracted by the apparent sexism of the phrase "great man." Wilde was a creature of his time, and your readers are creatures of theirs.

Historians have become more sensitive to gender. This is reflected not only in their intellectual interests but also in their historical writing. Years ago it might have been acceptable to say, for example, "The historian who conducts his research in an archive should ensure that he prepares himself well for his task." The masculine pronoun with an antecedent of indeterminate gender was conventional. Today, such a construction seems not only biased but inaccurate, given how many historians are women. To avoid such sexist pitfalls, you have several options for how to change the sentence. One is to include both masculine and feminine genders, although this alteration can create very long sentences: "The historian who conducts his or her research in an archive should ensure that he or she prepares himself or herself well for his or her task." Simpler solutions should be considered. You could try using neutral pronouns such as "everyone," "anybody," or "one." This alleviates the problem with a lack of gender inclusivity, but it can end up sounding painfully contrived or pretentious: "The historian who conducts one's research in an archive should ensure that one prepares oneself well for one's task." You might find it better to pluralize the subject: "Historians who conduct their research in an archive should ensure that they prepare themselves well for their task." It is becoming increasingly common to use "they" as a singular pronoun, although not all readers will accept this as grammatically correct: "The historian who conducts their research in an archive should ensure that they prepare themselves well for their task." Often the simplest solution is to rearrange the sentence so as to avoid the gendered pronouns entirely: "The historian who conducts research in an archive should ensure adequate preparation for the task."

As a general principle, be respectful and inclusive in your choice of words, and be especially thoughtful when dealing with potentially sensitive or hurtful material.

Check for These Common Diction Problems

It is easy to misuse words and expressions, especially when you see them so often misused. Word-processing programs make it possible to search for any given word, and good dictionaries will help you understand how to use words correctly.

If you need further assistance on points of usage, ask a reference librarian to help you find an updated version of H.W. Fowler's classic work, *The New Fowler's Modern English Usage*. It is the basis for many of the entries in the following list of common problems that appear in historical writing. You may also wish to consult Margery Fee and Janice McAlpine, *Guide to Canadian English Usage*, Second Edition (Oxford: Oxford University Press, 2011).

Accept and **except** have very different meanings. "Accept" is a verb that means to receive or agree to something, while "except" is a preposition indicating that something is excluded or omitted. To keep the words separate in your mind, you might find it helpful to link "except" with "exclude."

AD and **BC** mean *Anno domini* [in the year of the Lord] and Before Christ, respectively. These abbreviations seem to be slipping out of use, in favour of CE and BCE, which mean Common Era and Before the Common Era. Both systems place year "0" at the same time, so that "33 AD" and "33 CE" are the same year. The CE/BCE dating system is especially helpful in world history courses or in any historical investigation in which diverse approaches to religion are considered.

Affect and **effect** can confuse students both as verbs and as nouns. As a verb, "to affect" means to influence, whereas "to effect" means to cause or result in. "Her strategy affected voter turn-out so much that it effected a change in government." "To affect" can also mean to pretend or to assume the false appearance of something, but this is a less common meaning. "He affected an enjoyment of his other subjects, but his true love was for history." As a noun, an "affect" is a feeling or mood, and an "effect" usually means a result. "His cheerful affect in the negotiations brought about the desired effect."

All right is proper for formal writing. Many people spell it as "alright," but most authorities regard this as overly casual.

All together and **altogether** do not mean the same thing. All together expresses a complete group, while altogether means completely or entirely. Here is a sentence to make the difference clear: "They went to the hockey game all together, but he was not altogether sure that it was a good idea."

And/or appears frequently in insecure writing, possibly because it has a legalistic sound to it. "And/or" is not incorrect, but it is inelegant. It implies that the two items joined together can be taken apart, which is a fundamentally odd concept. You can avoid it by writing "X or Y or both," or just by writing "or."

Ante- and **anti-** are two Latin prefixes that students often confuse. "*Ante*" means "before," whereas "*anti*" means "against." For example, "antebellum America" refers to the United States before the Civil War, whereas "antiwar protestors" were people who opposed a war.

Because is a word commonly used in historical writing because historians usually want to learn what caused things to happen. "Letitia Youmans founded the first Canadian local of the Women's Christian Temperance Union because she was distressed by the effects of alcohol on family life." Teachers sometimes tell students not to start a sentence with "because," and generally speaking they are right. "Because" introduces a clause that depends on another clause; if you reverse the order of the two clauses in the sentence about Letitia Youmans and start it with the "because" clause, the sentence would be harder to follow. Still, there are circumstances when historical writers make reasonable exceptions to this rule.

Cannot is usually written as one word, not as "can not." The contraction "can't" is usually too colloquial for academic writing.

Different is the subject of some debate. Some people will tell you that "different" can only be followed by "from," never by "than" or "to." The editors of the *Oxford English Dictionary* disagree. They point out that people have been using "different to" since 1526 and "different than" since 1644. That said, "different from" works best in most cases, especially in formal writing.

Double negatives are not uncommon in historical writing, but unless they are used carefully they can cause undue confusion. Two negatives always cancel each other out: "Benazir Bhutto was not displeased by the result of the vote" is a roundabout way of saying that she was at least somewhat pleased. Occasionally a double negative can add an ironic note, but a straightforward positive is usually best.

Due to might seem harmless enough, but generations of history professors have warned students against it. Strunk and White, in their classic *The Elements of Style*, explain that "due to" should be used only to mean "attributable to," as in "Custer's defeat was due to poor intelligence." It should not substitute for "because" or "through," as in "Custer lost the battle due to poor intelligence."

E.g. and **i.e.** are abbreviations for Latin phrases. "E.g." is short for "*exempli gratia,*" which means "for the sake of example." It can be used when you mean to say "for instance." "Visitors to the Chinese emperor's court enjoyed many different kinds of performance, e.g., plays, dances, and even opera." "I.e." is short for "*id est,*" which means "that is." It can be used when you mean to say "in other words." "Visitors to the Chinese emperor's court enjoyed music played on the lute's Chinese cousin, i.e., the pipa."

Its and **it's** are frequently confused. "Its" is the possessive form of "it": "When Castro lit a Montecristo, its pungent smoke filled the air." "It's" is the contraction of "it is": "It's not too late to learn how to write history." It is also worth mentioning that "it's," as a contraction, should generally not appear in formal writing.

Led is the past tense of "to lead." It may be true that "the First World War led to the Second World War," but don't confuse chronology with causation. It is true that 1939 followed 1914, but your readers will expect you to explain how the first war helped to cause the second war. Saying "led to" is often vague.

Novel is sometimes used by students to refer to any large book, even works of history. This is incorrect. By definition, a novel is a work of fiction.

Possessives are generally not difficult to form in English, but confusion often arises with words that end in the letter "s." You form the possessive of a singular noun by adding an apostrophe followed by an s. This is true even when the word ends in the letter s. For example, it is correct to write "King Charles's soldiers," or "the duchess's letters." There are some minor exceptions to this rule. Traditionally, ancient names ending in *s* take only an apostrophe, as in "Herodotus' writing." However, these constructions are sufficiently awkward that many writers form the possessive with "of," as in "the writing of Herodotus." You form the possessive of a plural noun that ends in an s by adding only an apostrophe: "The nurses' training." When a plural noun ends in a letter other than s, you form the possessive by adding an apostrophe and an s. "The women's march." Note that apostrophes are not used in forming the plural of abbreviations and numbers. "PCs were first manufactured in the 1980s."

Regard is misused frequently in compound prepositions like "with regards to" and "in regards to." There are two proper ways to use "regard." If it is part of a compound preposition, use the singular "regard," as in "with regard to" or "in regard to." If it is a verb, conjugate accordingly: "as it regards" or "as they regard."

That and **which** create much uncertainty among writers trying to choose between them. For most traditionalists, authors should use "that" in restrictive clauses, and "which" in nonrestrictive clauses. Here is an example of a sentence with a restrictive clause: "Despite the tense atmosphere that prevailed during the trial, Nelson Mandela spoke his mind to the court." The clause "prevailed during the trial" is essential to the statement "despite the tense atmosphere," and so "that" is used. Here is an example of a sentence with a nonrestrictive clause: "Apartheid, which had legally been in place since 1948, finally came to an end." The clause "which had legally been in place since 1948" is a parenthetical statement that might just as well be placed in another sentence, and so "which" is used.

Who, whose, and **whom** are different forms of the same relative pronoun. "Who" is the form for when you are using the word as the subject of a sentence or clause. "The captain who spotted the enemy vessel first was not yet ready to engage in battle." "Whose" is the possessive form. "Captain Cameron, whose vessel was still in dry dock, was nevertheless clear in his intent to lead." ("Who's" is a contraction of "who is" and, as a contraction, probably does not belong in your formal history essay.) "Whom" is used when the pronoun is the object of a verb or preposition. "The captain, whom the sailors nicknamed 'Caledonia' on account of his Scottish birth, was ready to fire. The officer to whom Caledonia gave the order did not hesitate."

Review

1. Choose your words carefully.
2. Avoid language that is overly pretentious or informal.
3. Call people and groups what they want to be called.
4. Be direct and say what you mean.

Notes

1. James Belich, *The Victorian Inter-pretation of Racial Conflict: The Maori, the British, and the New Zealand Wars* (Montreal and Kingston: McGill and Queen's University Press, 1989), 20–1.

2. George Orwell, "Politics and the English Language," in *Fields of Writing*, eds. Nancy Comley et al., 4th ed. (New York: St. Martin's Press, 1994), 618.

3. Susan Hill, *The Clay We Are Made Of: Haudenosaunee Land Tenure on the Grand River* (Winnipeg: University of Manitoba Press, 2017).

4. Micah A. Pawling, "*Wəlastəkwey* (Maliseet) Homeland: Waterscapes and Continuity within the Lower St John River Valley, 1784–1900," *Acadiensis* 46, 2 (Summer/Autumn 2017).

5. Oscar Wilde, "The Critic as Artist," published in *Intentions*, in The Complete Works of Oscar Wilde, volume 4, ed. Josephine M. Guy (Oxford: Oxford University Press, 2007), 145.

9

Revising and Editing

This guide is not a cookbook for historians, and there are no recipes for writing history. Historians share certain conventions, as this book has laid out, but every historian has his or her own way of writing. Approaches to any given writing project depend partly on the subject of the work and partly on personal style. The more you read, the more you will absorb a diverse repertoire of approaches. The more you write, the more you will gain a sense of your own style and interests. At the same time, you will become more familiar with where your own strengths and weaknesses lie. You have probably heard of the ancient Greek inscription over the temple at Delphi: "Know thyself." Get to know your own weaknesses as a writer, then watch out for them as you revise and edit.

Get Some Perspective

Once your draft is complete, it is important to get some distance from it before you start revising. You are writing for an audience, and to do that you must be able to see your writing as someone else sees it. Spend a few days working on other things, if you can, to put some distance between yourself and your writing. If you don't have a few days to spare, even an hour or two spent doing something else will help you see your paper as your readers will, with fresh eyes.

If you are lucky, you might have an instructor or friend who is willing to read a first draft and comment on it. A good critical assessment will point out both strengths and weaknesses in the work.

Take all the comments seriously: even if you're sure your paper includes something your reader thinks it lacks, the fact that the reader couldn't see it suggests that your expression was not as clear as you had hoped. Be careful how you proceed with this help, because too much assistance can venture into the territory of an academic offence. If someone other than you is writing the paper, then you should not be receiving credit for the work. To ensure that the paper you submit is your own, ask any helper to hold back from making changes. The helper may point out errors, but you should be the one who corrects them. The helper may tell you which sentences are confusing, or which arguments fail to persuade, but it is up to you, the writer, to make the changes that will improve the paper.

Revise Your Draft

Once you have gained some perspective on your writing, it is time to revise. If you have received feedback from an instructor or a friend already, begin by addressing your critic's comments. Write another draft that incorporates the suggested changes, then stand back from your paper and assess it again.

No critic, no matter how generous, will tell you everything you need to know to turn your draft into a prize-winning essay. You yourself must take responsibility for revising, and effective revising takes time. Your eye can tire easily while scrutinizing your own work, and it is impossible to catch every weakness, at every level, in just one reading. So a good, basic strategy for revising is to begin with broad revisions to the argument and structure of the paper as a whole, and then move on to sentence-level language issues. Proceeding from big to small issues in this way means that you can be sure your paper's argument and structure are sound before you start to polish each sentence. Finally, proofread for spelling, grammar, punctuation, and formatting.

Evaluate Your Arguments and Narratives

Check your paper to make sure your arguments are solidly and consistently sustained from the beginning to the end. Does the evidence support the inferences? Are all the inferences fully warranted? Does the argument flow and develop smoothly? Will readers find this to be an interesting and significant argument?

Check your paper to make sure your audience knows what they need to know in the correct order. Are terms, characters, and events introduced properly? Is the sequence of events clear? Have you included all the relevant details and eliminated extraneous information that does not drive any of the main stories?

Check your paper to make sure you have established a consistent voice as a narrator. Do you maintain the same vantage point as omniscient or uncertain? Do you treat cause and consequence, continuity and change intelligently in every section?

When evaluating these aspects of your writing, you should be focusing on the big picture of structure and content. Concentrate on the introduction, topic sentences, and conclusion, because these are where the main points should be laid out. A good way to ensure that your thesis aligns with your evidence and analysis throughout the whole paper is to create a reverse outline. First, write the main idea of each paragraph in the margin beside that paragraph. You need to be a bit severe at this point: record what is actually in the paragraph, not what you meant to say. Once you have done this for each paragraph, you will have extracted the main points from the paper and created an outline in the margins. Next, read through this reverse outline to ensure that the structure is solid. Does every paragraph relate directly to the main argument? If one of your paragraphs does not relate to the main argument, remove it from the paper. If you can't bear to delete it, put it aside by moving it into a different file so that it can be saved for a future paper. If most of your paragraphs actually contradict the main argument, adjust the main argument so that it matches the evidence. Is each paragraph centred around one main idea? If there are two or three main ideas in a paragraph, split that paragraph into several. Are ideas scattered through multiple paragraphs? If the same idea is repeated several times in non-sequential paragraphs, rearrange the structure of the paper to consolidate these repetitions into a single section.

Evaluate Your Sentences and Word Choices

Once you are satisfied with the structure and arguments of your paper, read through it again to focus on sentences and words. Try to see your sentences as your readers will. Have you chosen strong verbs? Is the order of ideas appropriate? Does every sentence follow smoothly from the one before it and develop a new idea?

Also look at your word choices, or diction, and try to see these as your readers will. Are you writing in a precise language that your audience will understand? Have you defined specialized terms that may be unfamiliar to your readers?

When evaluating the sentences and words of your writing, you should be focusing on the language itself. For many people, it is easier to see errors on the page than on the screen, so try printing out a hard copy of your paper. If you are seriously committed to knowing what your writing will sound like to a reader, print out two copies and give one to a friend or colleague. Ask them to read it out loud to you, while you follow along on your own copy. Any time that the reader sounds confused, or stumbles, or emphasizes the wrong thing, make a note of it in your copy. After the reading is complete, go back to each place where you have noted a discrepancy between what you meant to say and how your reader said it, and revise until you and the reader are in agreement.

Proofread the Final Draft

Proofreading is an essential stage in the writing process. If your writing is stained with mistakes, no matter how minor, even your most brilliant ideas will come across as sloppy and unkempt. Proofreading takes time and patience. Chances are that by the time you start, you will already have read your paper so many times that your eyes will start to wander. Be disciplined. Force yourself to read every line and every word. If this gets too boring, put the writing aside for a short time and come back to it later. You might even try reading the paragraphs in reverse order, so that you focus less on the argument and narrative and more on the word-by-word language. There is no real way to make proofreading interesting for most people, but still it must be done.

1. Proofread for Punctuation. Punctuation helps to guide the pace of reading, and it supplies cues for what the writer wants to emphasize. More fundamentally, punctuation clarifies a sentence's meaning. Consider how the following sentences change meaning depending on punctuation:

> A woman without her man is nothing.
> A woman: without her, man is nothing.
> He finds inspiration in cooking his family and his dog.
> He finds inspiration in cooking, his family, and his dog.
> Watch out for the man eating shark!
> Watch out for the man-eating shark!

Imprecise or incorrect punctuation can cause problems with your writing. If you have trouble with punctuation, refer to *The Chicago Manual of Style* or other writing manuals for guidance.

2. Proofread for Spelling. The spell-checking feature on your word-processing program will catch most spelling mistakes, but not all of them. Homonyms (words that sound the same but mean different things) are especially likely to escape notice: to / two / too; there / their / they're; and lead / led are among the more commonly misspelled words. Proper names of people and places should also be double-checked in the proofreading process, because your credibility as a writer of history will certainly suffer if you repeatedly spell the names of historical figures and historians incorrectly.

Some spelling variations are not errors, but choices. Canadian, British, and US English follow different conventions for certain words. "Realise" and "gaol" in Britain are "realize" and "jail" in Canada and the US; "color" and "theater" in the US are "colour" and "theatre" in Canada and Britain. Follow whichever system you are instructed to use, and be consistent. If you are asked to use Canadian spellings in particular, consult *The Canadian Oxford Dictionary*.

3. Read Your Paper Aloud. Reading aloud is an old trick for catching writing problems, because it forces you to review every word. Others may think you are eccentric, but your readers will appreciate the end result: a better piece of writing.

Check the Formatting

Professors sometimes have their own preferences for how to format and present your paper. Pay careful attention to any instructions you are given regarding font and layout. If you have not received any specific directions, use a consistent and simple format throughout the paper to avoid distractions. Typically, your readers will prefer a plain font in a reasonable size (12-point Times font is a good choice) with one-inch margins and lines double-spaced. Number all the pages, beginning with page 1 on your first page of text. If you are asked for a title page, include on it your name, the title of your paper, the name of your professor or teaching assistant, and the date of submission. If you are not asked for a title page, include this same information on the first page of your paper.

Submit Your Paper

Leave yourself enough time to take the final steps before submission, whether you need to print up a hard copy or upload an electronic version. Deadlines are deadlines; if a paper is late, whatever the reason, it is susceptible to a late penalty.

Look over the paper once more to make sure everything is in the right place. Save a copy of your notes, rough drafts, and final product in case you are asked to produce them. Then submit your paper and enjoy the feeling that someone will soon be reading your writing about history.

Review

1. Take a break to give yourself some perspective.
2. Revise several times, changing your focus from broad to narrow.
3. Proofread carefully.
4. Verify formatting requirements.
5. Keep all notes and drafts, and save a copy of your work.
6. Submit and rejoice!

Revise Your Draft(s)
-Is the argument consistent and logically organized?
-Are the inferences valid?
-Is the evidence sufficient?
-Are all paragraphs well structured?
-Is the language clear and precise?

Proofread Your Draft
-Are all sentences without error?
-Does the formatting match the instructions?
-Have notes and drafts been saved?

Flowchart Chapter 9 Writing your final draft

Appendix A

Different Kinds of
History Assignments

Most of this book is written to help students write a historical research essay. This is probably the most common assignment in history courses, but there are other kinds of assignments that you may encounter as well, either as steps toward the research essay or as stand-alone projects.

Primary Source Analysis

Instructors often assign a primary source analysis to give students the opportunity to conduct primary research, practise the close reading of a text, and establish a more immediate sense of connection to the past than what research using secondary sources can provide.

The analysis of a primary source demands that you bring your critical abilities to bear. All historical documents, public as well as private, were produced by real people who were influenced by the times and places in which they lived, as well as by their own experiences. This means that you need to keep the context of the source's creation in mind as you read. Your instructor will not be looking simply for a summary of what the document says, but rather for a thoughtful analysis of what it means and what it can tell us about people, places, and events. The simplest way to approach a primary source analysis is to follow the "question" model outlined in Chapter 2. You won't always be able to answer every question suggested here, and sometimes the answers—the whys and hows, or the wheres and whens—will overlap. Still, posing the questions will help you to think carefully about your source.

The assignment's instructions may limit your research to just the primary source under study. In this case, where you can draw evidence only from the primary source itself, you will need to think carefully about what the source can and cannot tell you. If the instructions tell you to read secondary sources alongside the primary source, use these to help you with context and interpretation.

A good dictionary will help you understand any archaic or extremely formal language that might be in your source. If the document is very old, consult the full-length *Oxford English Dictionary* (as opposed to the various shorter and "concise" editions), which gives the history of a word's usage as well as current meanings. Most libraries have a subscription to the full online version.

Book or Article Review

When writing a book or article review, your main task is to provide a critical analysis. A review is not merely, or even primarily, a summary; it is an evaluation of what the book or article contributes to our understanding of history. It should consider the book or article's theme and purpose, its evidence and arguments, and its conclusions and significance.

A book review is not the same as a book report. If you have never written an academic book review before, you may find it helpful to look at examples in scholarly journals such as *The Canadian Historical Review*, *The American Historical Review*, or *The Journal of World History*. The first step is obvious: read the book. There is no substitute for careful and thoughtful reading of the entire work, although it is definitely useful to scan the introduction, chapter headings, and conclusion up front. As you read, note the author's main points and your observations of the evidence and arguments, as well as any short passages that you may want to quote in your review.

Once you have read the book, you can plan your approach. Does the assignment require you to look at other sources to put the book into a wider context? Are you supposed to link this book to the themes or materials of your course, or simply to review it according to your own evaluation of its merits? If you do further reading, pay attention to matters relating to the book's main arguments and evidence, especially if other sources emphasize significant ideas or events that your book seems to skim over or ignore. Also think about the criteria you will use to evaluate it.

Your personal response to the book—what you liked or didn't like about it—is not irrelevant, but your responsibility as a reviewer is to judge the strength of the book's arguments and evidence, identify its strengths and weaknesses, and assess its contribution to the field. If you are evaluating the book on its own merits, try to place it in the context of the themes and materials you are studying in your course.

Typically, a review will begin with a bibliographical reference that lists the author, title, and publication information for the work under review. Unless you have been instructed otherwise, summarize the work briefly, being careful to focus on the main points and the relevant evidence. This would also be a good place to mention the author's background and qualifications: whether the author is a professional historian, has specific expertise in the area, or has written other books on this or related subjects. You could also mention the arrangement of the book's contents, any additional features such as illustrations, and the style of writing. Keep these details brief, though; you want to leave as much space as possible for substantive discussion of the book's contents.

The body of the review will present your assessment of the book's arguments, evidence, and conclusion. Consider whether the author has achieved his or her goal and whether you are convinced by the arguments. You may include some quotations from the book, as long as they are short, relevant to your point, and representative of the book's contents, tone, and ideas. Just be sure not to take any quotation out of context—otherwise you run the risk of misrepresenting the author's meaning—and never quote anything just for the sake of quoting.

The last component of any book review is the conclusion. In this paragraph, summarize your main points, give your overall assessment of the book, and (if appropriate to the assignment) make a recommendation to your reader.

Throughout the writing process, remember that your job is to give your readers a clear, balanced idea of the book as a whole. Don't focus on one area of the work while ignoring other equally significant areas. And don't feel that you have to find something negative to say in order to fulfill your role as a critic. No book is perfect, and it's perfectly legitimate to note flaws if you find them, but you should be equally ready to praise the book's strengths. Finally, be sure to back up both your praise and your criticism with specific examples.

A second type of book review assignment, the comparative book review, requires you to compare two or more different books. If your professor leaves the selection of books to you, look for examples that bear some relationship to one another. Two biographies of Louis Riel would obviously work well for this type of essay, but one on Riel himself and another on Canadian federal policy towards Indigenous peoples in the nineteenth century might also allow you to make some useful commentary.

Once you have selected your books, go through them and note any points of similarity or difference, agreement or disagreement. Are there areas where one book sheds light on the other? Of course you won't be able to discuss everything the two authors say: just pick out the most significant areas. Now you can consider how to organize your review.

Start as before, with full bibliographical references, an introduction, and a short description of each book. Now there are two ways to proceed: you can discuss each book in its own section and then compare some of their points, or you can organize your paper thematically and compare the books directly, point by point. One way to choose between these approaches is to consider how directly the two works can be compared. If you have books with related but not identical subjects, can you find more than one or two significant elements to compare directly? If not, it might be easier to go with option number one (each book in its own section). If you can find significant points that are directly comparable, then you might choose option number two (point-by-point comparison).

A third common review assignment concentrates on one or more articles as opposed to books. The overall task is the same, but you will most likely be given fewer pages to work with. In this case it is crucial to keep your summary of the articles short so that you have adequate space for analytical comments.

Annotated Bibliography

An annotated bibliography is a list and brief description of sources that you are using in your research. It may be either a stand-alone project or a first step towards a research paper. As with a bibliography that goes at the end of the paper, arrange the list of sources alphabetically by author's last name and include the full bibliographic information for each item formatted according to *The Chicago Manual of Style*. In addition to the bibliographic information, provide also for each item a concise summary of the source, including its main argument or contribution to the field; a brief assessment of its strengths and limitations; and an indication of its value or relevance to your research project.

Historiographical Paper

Historiography is the study of how history is written—in effect, how historians shape history through their work. Thus a historiography paper generally takes a topic that has generated continuing interest and explores how historians have written about it.

History is not static. Interpretations of the past change because, as John H. Arnold points out, "History is above all else an argument. It is an argument between different historians; and, perhaps, an argument between the past and present."[1]

Historians do not generally strive for "the right answer." They strive to interpret the available evidence as fully and accurately as they can. Even when working with exactly the same evidence, their opinions frequently differ. Historians' interests and approaches also reflect their own times and circumstances. In the 1960s and 1970s, historians responded to the growth of feminist activism with a new interest in the history of women as a separate topic from the history of men. More recently, with the discussion of gay rights in Canada, interest in queer history has increased. Recent years have also seen growing interest in local history, the history of childhood, and environmental history.

What kinds of subjects might be suitable for a historiographical paper? Any topic that has been controversial or that historians have revisited in different ways over time would be suitable. It is also possible to write a historiographical paper about a particular historian, tracing the development of his or her work.

Typically, a historiographical paper will focus on how historians' approaches, themes, and questions have developed over the years and from place to place, providing insight into the historians and their times as well as the historical topic under discussion. Look for continuing or recurring themes, new themes and reassessments of old themes, and agreements and disagreements. The point is not particularly to review or critique the works or historians in question, although you could well include some comments along these lines. Rather, the point is to examine change over time, to analyze how and why historians' methods, interests, and approaches have changed. You might also consider the direction in which the historiography of your topic is likely to develop in the future. For instance, if your paper is focused on the historiography of the energy industry in Canada, and you are aware of recent debates on oil and gas pipelines, you might speculate that environmental historians will soon be paying a lot of attention to this topic. A chronological organization usually works well for historiographical papers, but you could modify this format to discuss sub-themes such as the influence of gender or ethnicity on the writing of history.

Reading Response Journal

A reading journal assignment allows you to develop your own thoughts about course materials without the constraints that come with an essay assignment, although some instructors assign reading journals as bases for later papers. Unless otherwise instructed, you can use informal language and your own approach and arrangement, and you can let your thoughts run free. Keep some guidelines in mind, however. If your instructor is to read some or all of your material, make sure that your language is clean, your thoughts focused, and your points clear. This assignment is about thinking, not random musing.

Briefly summarize the reading, ensuring that you identify the most important points, any contentious points, and any points you do not understand. If you are responding to more than one piece, think about any similarities and differences of focus and opinion and consider the reasons for the differences.

If appropriate to the assignment, you might (within limits) consider your own reactions: for example, do you find the material interesting, dull, surprising, amusing, upsetting, intriguing? Why do you feel this way? Emotional responses can be interesting, and you may certainly include them (unless your instructor rules them out). Keep in mind, though, that responses based on historical knowledge, on other reading, or on experience are probably more relevant.

Try to set aside a regular time for your journal. It may be tempting to let the journal slide when you have more immediate deadlines, but you will regret putting the journal work off when you have to catch up on it several weeks or months later. You will not be able to do a good and thoughtful job under those circumstances. Besides, the whole point of a response journal is to record your thinking as it develops over time and help you to consolidate your understanding of the materials as the course progresses. Writing several weeks' worth of journal entries all at once defeats the purpose and deprives you of the benefits.

Research Proposal

A research proposal can be a very useful exercise. If submitted before you begin writing a more extensive essay, it gives you the opportunity to start work in good time, to think carefully about your topic, and to get feedback from your instructor when it is most useful. Just keep in mind that a research proposal is not as easy as it may at first appear. It will probably require a short description of your research topic and its significance. It may also ask you to outline the main points and structure of your essay. Allow yourself plenty of time to think about a topic, find relevant sources, and read them in enough detail to know how they relate to your project and to each other. Thoughtful and careful work on this now will ease the writing process later, and allow you to benefit from your instructor's help along the way.

Oral Presentation

Many students find the very thought of doing a presentation nerve-wracking, but presenting can be an excellent way of sharing your research with others.

A good presentation requires planning. First, consider your audience. If you are presenting in your class, then you can presume that your audience with be familiar with the course material, but you will need to give them some background on your specific topic so that they can follow your arguments and appreciate your analysis. Provide all necessary dates, places, names, and definitions for unfamiliar terms.

Remember that people listening to a presentation don't absorb information exactly the same way as do readers of a paper. In a presentation, you control the pace, and members of your audience can't take a break and find a dictionary if they need to look up an unfamiliar word or go back to review a section if they need to refresh their memory. Build your presentation around a strong and simple structure, repeat important points if necessary, and give very clear signals about what you're saying and why. If you are going to provide three examples of something to prove a point, listeners will appreciate some help in keeping track—by hearing you say "Three examples prove [this point] well. The first is. . . . The second example to prove [the point] is. . . . And as a final example. . . ." You will probably find that you need to be selective in providing examples because of time constraints. If you are trying to figure out how much you can say in a given length of time, a good rule of thumb is that one page of double-spaced text takes a little over two minutes to read at a comfortable pace.

Practise your presentation several times before giving it. If you can, practise it in front of people. Have them time you, and ask them if anything was unclear. Find for yourself a comfortable posture, including somewhere to rest your hands, and make regular eye contact with people in the room. Put some notes in front of you if you worry that you'll forget important points or veer off track, but try to give the presentation without reading a script.

Follow any instructions you were given about content and form. Are you supposed to use slides? If so, make sure that any writing on them is clear, and include citations for texts and images. Can you give handouts? If so, this might be a good place to put key dates, maps, a glossary of terms, and a list of suggested readings.

When the time comes for the presentation itself, keep in mind that everyone in the room is there at that moment to hear what you have to say. Don't be upset if you feel a bit nervous—this is normal and can actually help inject some energy into your delivery.

Poster

Research posters are typically set up at conferences or seminars so that researchers can share their findings with a wide general audience. Basically, posters are meant to advertise research and invite further discussion. Viewers walking by can look at the posters on display and ask the researchers questions about their work. In putting together a poster, therefore, find a design that will encourage and facilitate conversation. Make the poster visually appealing, easy to read, and to the point. All the important information should be readable from several metres away, and the text should be brief and direct. Visual elements like pictures, tables, and graphs should be prominent. At the poster presentation, stand beside your poster. Be prepared to present a brief oral introduction to your research and to answer questions.

Final Examination

Most history courses conclude with a final examination, and a little planning can help a lot when the time comes to write it.

Watch for recurring themes, ideas, people, or events frequently emphasized by the book or instructor, and focus on these when studying. An especially useful study method is to compose your own questions and then write model answers to them. For example, if a major course theme has been the development of federal–provincial relations in the nineteenth century, you could compose a question about the shifting power dynamics between the two levels of government. Then you could decide on and study the major "sign-post" events and factors to discuss, such as the rise of the provincial rights movement, the New Brunswick schools questions of the 1870s, the Ontario boundary dispute of the 1880s, the Northwest Rebellion, the formation of the *Parti national*, the Manitoba schools question, and the Laurier–Greenway compromise. Your question will probably not be identical to anything on the exam paper, but you will almost certainly have studied in detail the material necessary to answer the question that does appear.

Try not to leave your studying until the last moment. Set aside a regular time to study and review, then keep to your schedule. Obviously, you are more likely to do well if you have worked hard all term and studied diligently for the exam. Apart from any other benefit, this will give you the confidence you need to get a good sleep the night before the exam and arrive well rested.

When you get the exam, don't just jump in and start writing. Take a few moments to read the script carefully. Pay attention to any directions regarding the length or format of your answers. Think about how much time you have and assign a ballpark time limit to each part of the exam so that you will not feel overly rushed. Identify the easiest questions, and if you can answer them very quickly, do that now. If there are some that will be easy but will need a little time to compose, set them aside.

Next, look at the rest of the questions. If you think some will be really difficult, set them aside as well and just let them percolate in the back of your brain for a while. You may find that, as you relax into the exam, you will start remembering things that you thought you had forgotten. In the meantime, complete the questions that are neither the easiest nor the hardest. Then go back to the easy ones, but resist any temptation to spend too much time or space on the answers just because you know them so well. Finally, turn to the hardest questions. Following this approach allows you to use your time effectively and ensure that you don't leave any "easy" marks on the table.

If there is an essay component to the final exam, read each question carefully and think about what a thorough but focused answer needs to cover. Take a few moments to write a brief outline. Remember that every essay requires an introduction and conclusion, a thesis statement, logical ordering of points, and sufficient evidence to support your arguments. Focus on the question in front of you: don't try to change it into a question you can answer more easily, and don't pad your answer with a lot of unnecessary information just because you know it. You need to show your instructor that you understand the material so well that you are not just able to regurgitate but to develop your own thoughts based on all the evidence. Leave a few minutes to proofread at the end to make sure that both your ideas and your handwriting are clear.

Above all, have confidence and remember that an exam is a chance to show how much you know. Your professor will be looking for the correct answers to straightforward factual questions, of course, but also for evidence that you have thought about the material and made it your own.

Notes

1. John H. Arnold, *History: A Very Short Introduction* (Oxford: Oxford University Press, 2000), 13.

Appendix B

Citation Guide

Most history assignments will require you to reference your sources by using footnotes or endnotes and a bibliography formatted according to the system laid out in *The Chicago Manual of Style*.

Notes

Footnotes and endnotes tell your readers where you got the information that is presented in your paper. You must provide a note every time you refer to someone else's material or ideas, whether this is through quotation, paraphrase, or summary.

Create a note with a **superscript number** in the text. Start with number 1 at the beginning of the paper and keep going: don't start again with number 1 at the top of each page (or the beginning of each new section), and don't use the same number every time you refer to the same source. Each superscript number refers your reader to an accompanying reference note either at the bottom of the page (a footnote) or on a separate page at the end of the paper (an endnote).

Note references are usually placed at the end of the sentence: "J.R. Miller argues that the First Nations peoples in Canada consistently sought to determine their own paths.[4]" The number belongs at the end of the sentence, rather than following Miller's name, because the entire sentence concerns his book *Skyscrapers Hide the Heavens*, 3rd ed. (Toronto: University of Toronto Press, 2000). The most usual time when it might be appropriate to place the note in the middle of a sentence would be if the latter part of the sentence referred to a second author and it was necessary to distinguish the two. If no confusion would exist, there is no problem putting multiple sources into one note; just enter them in the same order in which you used them in the sentence and separate them with semicolons.

The first time you refer to a given work, provide the author's name, title, and publishing information in full. For subsequent notes referring to the same work, use just the author's last name and a shortened title. Always provide page numbers indicating exactly where the information is found. When you see "Ibid." in notes, it is short for the Latin *ibidem*, meaning "the same."

It indicates that the information in this note is exactly the same as the information in the note immediately preceding it.

The only difference between footnotes and endnotes is their placement: footnotes are placed at the bottom of each page, and endnotes are placed at the end of the paper. They are otherwise formatted identically. They should contain all the information necessary for readers to locate the sources of your information.

Bibliographies

The bibliography is placed at the end of the paper. It should contain all the sources that were consulted in the preparation of the paper, arranged alphabetically by authors' last names. The first line of each entry is placed at the left-hand margin, while second and subsequent lines are indented.

Citation Examples

The following examples show how to format notes (either footnotes or endnotes) and bibliography entries for different kinds of sources. For anything not covered here (including videos, blogs, unpublished dissertations, personal communications), see Chapter 14 of *The Chicago Manual of Style*.

A book with a single author
In a note

#. First Name Last Name, *Title* (City of publication: Publisher, Year of publication), page(s).

5. David Campbell, *It Can't Last Forever: The 19th Battalion and the Canadian Corps in the First World War* (Waterloo: Wilfrid Laurier University Press, 2017), 42.

6. Santhi Kavuri-Bauer, *Monumental Matters: The Power, Subjectivity, and Space of India's Mughal Architecture* (Durham: Duke University Press, 2011), 37.

In a shortened note

> 7. Kavuri-Bauer, *Monumental Matters*, 89–101.
>
> 8. Campbell, *It Can't Last Forever*, 42.

In a bibliography

> Last Name, First Name. *Title.* City of publication: Publisher, Year of publication.
>
> Campbell, David. *It Can't Last Forever: The 19th Battalion and the Canadian Corps in the First World War.* Waterloo: Wilfrid Laurier University Press, 2017.
>
> Kavuri-Bauer, Santhi. *Monumental Matters: The Power, Subjectivity, and Space of India's Mughal Architecture.* Durham: Duke University Press, 2011.

A book with multiple authors
In a note

> 9. Robert Bothwell and J.L. Granatstein, *Our Century: The Canadian Journey in the Twentieth Century* (Toronto: McArthur, 2000), 53–56.
>
> 10. Alex Lichtenstein and Rick Halpern, *Margaret Bourke-White and the Dawn of Apartheid* (Bloomington: Indiana University Press, 2016), 100–102.

In a shortened note

> 11. Bothwell and Granatstein, *Our Century*, 93.
>
> 12. Lichtenstein and Halpern, *Margaret Bourke-White*, 56–58.

In a bibliography

> Bothwell, Robert, and J.L. Granatstein. *Our Century: The Canadian Journey in the Twentieth Century.* Toronto: McArthur, 2000.
>
> Lichtenstein, Alex, and Rick Halpern. *Margaret Bourke-White and the Dawn of Apartheid.* Bloomington: Indiana University Press, 2016.

An anonymous work

When the author is unknown, the note and bibliography entry should begin with the title of the work. For the purposes of alphabetizing the bibliography, ignore the initial article ("a," "an," "the," etc.).

In a note

13. *A Short Authentic Account of the Expedition against Quebec in the Year 1759, Under Command of a Major-General James Wolfe. By a Volunteer upon That Expedition* (Quebec: Middleton & Dawson, 1872), 13–15.

14. *Memorial for the Booksellers of Edinburgh and Glasgow, Relating to the Process against Them by Some of the London Booksellers; Which Depended before the Court of Session, and Is Now under Appeal* (Edinburgh, 1765?), 1–3.

In a shortened note

15. *Memorial for the Booksellers of Edinburgh and Glasgow*, 2.

16. *A Short Authentic Account of the Expedition against Quebec in the Year 1759*, 16.

In a bibliography

Memorial for the Booksellers of Edinburgh and Glasgow, Relating to the Process against Them by Some of the London Booksellers; Which Depended before the Court of Session, and Is Now under Appeal. Edinburgh, [1765?].

A Short Authentic Account of the Expedition against Quebec in the Year 1759, Under Command of a Major-General James Wolfe. By a Volunteer upon That Expedition. Quebec: Middleton & Dawson, 1872.

A revised edition

In a note

17. Sheila Fitzpatrick, *The Russian Revolution*, 4th ed. (Oxford: Oxford University Press, 2017), 19–25.

18. Don Morrow and Kevin B. Warmsley, *Sport in Canada: A History*, 3rd ed. (Toronto: Oxford University Press, 2013), 21–22.

In a shortened note

>19. Fitzpatrick, *Russian Revolution*, 103.

>20. Morrow and Warmsley, *Sport in Canada*, 89.

In a bibliography

>Fitzpatrick, Sheila. *The Russian Revolution*. 4th ed. Oxford: Oxford University Press, 2017.

>Morrow, Don and Kevin B. Warmsley. *Sport in Canada: A History.* 3rd ed. Toronto: Oxford University Press, 2013.

An edited book

In a note

>21. Gerald Hallowell, ed., *The Oxford Companion to Canadian History* (Toronto: Oxford University Press, 2004), 23–111.

>22. Zhou Xun, ed., *The Great Famine in China, 1958–1962: A Documentary History* (New Haven: Yale University Press, 2012), 11–15, 35.

In a shortened note

>23. Hallowell, *The Oxford Companion to Canadian History,* 24.

>24. Xun, *The Great Famine in China*, 73.

In a bibliography

>Hallowell, Gerald, ed. *The Oxford Companion to Canadian History*. Toronto: Oxford University Press, 2004.

>Xun, Zhou, ed. *The Great Famine in China, 1958–1962: A Documentary History*. New Haven: Yale University Press, 2012.

A translated book

In a note

>25. Marie de l'Incarnation, *From Mother to Son: The Selected Letters of Marie de l'Incarnation to Claude Martin*, trans. Mary Dunn (Oxford: Oxford University Press, 2014), 54–58.

>26. *The Palace Law of Ayutthaya and the Thammasat: Law and Kingship in Siam*, ed. and trans. Chris Baker and Pasuk

Phongpaichit (Ithaca: Southeast Asia Program Publications, Cornell University Press, 2016), 125–43.

In a shortened note

27. Marie de l'Incarnation, *From Mother to Son*, 67.

28. *The Palace Law of Ayutthaya and the Thammasat*, 285–301.

In a bibliography

Marie de l'Incarnation. *From Mother to Son: The Selected Letters of Marie de L'Incarnation to Claude Martin*. Translated by Mary Dunn. Oxford: Oxford University Press, 2014.

The Palace Law of Ayutthaya and the Thammasat: Law and Kingship in Siam. Edited and translated by Chris Baker and Pasuk Phongpaichit. Ithaca: Southeast Asia Program Publications, Cornell University Press, 2016.

A chapter or section in a book

In a note

#. First Name Last Name, "Chapter Title," in *Book Title*, ed. First Name Last Name (City of publication: Publisher, year), page(s).

29. John Borrows, "Indigenous Constitutionalism: Pre-existing Legal Genealogies in Canada," in *The Oxford Handbook of the Canadian Constitution*, ed. Peter Oliver, Patrick Macklem, and Natalie Des Rosiers (New York: Oxford University Press, 2017), 13–14.

30. Abderrahman Ayoub, "The Arab Folklorist in a Postcolonial Period," in *Beyond Colonialism and Nationalism in the Maghrib: History, Culture and Politics*, ed. Ali Abdullatif Ahmida (New York: Palgrave Macmillan, 2009), 35–36.

In a shortened note

31. Borrows, "Indigenous Constitutionalism," 14–15.

32. Ayoub, "The Arab Folklorist," 37.

In a bibliography

> Last Name, First Name. "Chapter Title." In *Book Title*, edited by First Name Last Name, page range of section. City of publication: Publisher, year.

> Ayoub, Abderrahman. "The Arab Folklorist in a Postcolonial Period." In *Beyond Colonialism and Nationalism in the Maghrib: History, Culture and Politics*, edited by Ali Abdullatif Ahmida, 35–47. New York: Palgrave Macmillan, 2009.

> Borrows, John. "Indigenous Constitutionalism: Pre-existing Legal Genealogies in Canada." In *The Oxford Handbook of the Canadian Constitution*, edited by Peter Oliver, Patrick Macklem, and Natalie Des Rosiers, 13–43. New York: Oxford University Press, 2017.

A document in an anthology

In a note

> 33. "Minutes of Directors of Compagnie du Nord, 1684," in *The French Regime in the Upper Country of Canada During the Seventeenth Century*, ed. Cornelius J. Jaenen (Toronto: The Champlain Society, 1996), 208.

> 34. Friedrich Spee, "A Condemnation of Torture, 1631," in *The Witchcraft Sourcebook*, ed. Brian P. Levack (New York: Routledge, 2004), 145.

In a shortened note

> 35. "Minutes of Directors of Compagnie du Nord," 210.
> 36. Spee, "A Condemnation of Torture," 146–47.

In a bibliography

> "Minutes of Directors of Compagnie du Nord, 1684." In *The French Regime in the Upper Country of Canada During the Seventeenth Century*, edited by Cornelius J. Jaenen, 208–11. Toronto: The Champlain Society, 1996.

> Spee, Friedrich. "A Condemnation of Torture, 1631." In *The Witchcraft Sourcebook*, edited by Brian P. Levack, 145–52. New York: Routledge, 2004.

An e-book

When you consult a book online, include the URL, name of the database, or format. If no fixed page numbers are available, provide the title of a section or another number in the notes, or omit if not available.

In a note

> 37. Lesley Erickson, *Westward Bound: Sex, Violence, the Law, and the Making of a Settler Society* (Vancouver: UBC Press, 2011), 38–39, https://books-scholarsportal-info.myaccess.library.utoronto.ca/en/read?id=/ebooks/ebooks3/upress/2013-08-25/1/9780774818605.

> 38. George Hamandishe Karekwaivanane, *The Struggle over State Power in Zimbabwe: Law and Politics since 1950* (Cambridge: Cambridge University Press, 2017), 20–43, Cambridge Core.

In a shortened note

> 39. Erickson, *Westward Bound*, 42.

> 40. Karekwaivanane, *The Struggle over State Power in Zimbabwe*, 108.

In a bibliography

> Erickson, Lesley. *Westward Bound: Sex, Violence, the Law, and the Making of a Settler Society*. Vancouver: UBC Press, 2011. https://books-scholarsportal-info.myaccess.library.utoronto.ca/en/read?id=/ebooks/ebooks3/upress/2013-08-25/1/9780774818605.

> Karekwaivanane, George Hamandishe. *The Struggle over State Power in Zimbabwe: Law and Politics since 1950*. Cambridge: Cambridge University Press, 2017. Cambridge Core.

A journal article with one author

In a note

> #. First Name Last Name, "Title of Article," *Title of Journal* Volume, no. Issue (Publication date): page(s).

> 41. Carl Benn, "Missed Opportunities and the Problem of Mohawk Chief John Norton's Cherokee Ancestry,"

Ethnohistory 59, no. 2 (April, 2012): 261–62, https://doi-org.
myaccess.library.utoronto.ca/10.1215/00141801-1536885.

42. William Beik, "The Absolutism of Louis XIV as Social
Collaboration," *Past & Present* 188, no. 1 (August, 2005):
200–201.

In a shortened note

43. Benn, "Missed Opportunities," 263–64.

44. Beik, "The Absolutism of Louis XIV," 203.

In a bibliography

Last Name, First Name. "Title of Article." *Title of Journal*
Volume, no. Issue (Publication date): pages of article. If you
are using an online version, include the DOI (Digital Object
Identifier).

Beik, William. "The Absolutism of Louis XIV as Social Collaboration." *Past & Present* 188, no. 1 (August, 2005): 195–224.

Benn, Carl. "Missed Opportunities and the Problem of
Mohawk Chief John Norton's Cherokee Ancestry." *Ethnohistory* 59, no. 2 (April, 2012): 261–91. https://doi-org.
myaccess.library.utoronto.ca/10.1215/00141801-1536885.

A journal article with multiple authors

When a journal article has two or three authors, list them in the
same order as they appear in the publication. For four or more
authors, list up to ten in the bibliography, and in the note list only
the first followed by *et al.* (a Latin abbreviation for "and others").
If there are more than ten authors listed, list the first seven followed by *et al.*

In a note

45. Catherine Desbarats and Allan Greer, "Où est la
Nouvelle-France?" *Revue d'histoire de l'Amérique française* 64,
no. 3–4 (2011): 31–32.

46. Nicola Di Cosmo et al., "Environmental Stress and
Steppe Nomads: Rethinking the History of the Uyghur Empire

(744–840) with Paleoclimate Data," *Journal of Interdisciplinary History* 48, no. 4 (Spring, 2018): 439–40, https://doi.org/10.1162/JINH_a_01194.

In a shortened note

47. Di Cosmo et al., "Environmental Stress and Steppe Nomads," 441.

48. Desbarats and Greer, "Où est la Nouvelle-France," 33.

In a bibliography

Di Cosmo, Nicola, Amy Hessl, Caroline Leland, Oyunsanaa Byambasuren, Hanqin Tian, Baatarbileg Nachin, Neil Pederson, Laia Andreu-Hayles, and Edward R. Cook. "Environmental Stress and Steppe Nomads: Rethinking the History of the Uyghur Empire (744–840) with Paleoclimate Data." *Journal of Interdisciplinary History* 48, no. 4 (Spring, 2018): 439–63. https://doi.org/10.1162/JINH_a_01194.

Desbarats, Catherine and Allan Greer. "Où est la Nouvelle-France?" *Revue d'histoire de l'Amérique française* 64, no. 3–4 (2011): 31–62.

A news or magazine article

Articles from newspapers, online news sites, magazines, and blogs are cited in similar fashion. If the source was consulted online, include a URL or the name of the database in the citation.

In a note

49. Gordon M. Sayre, "The 'Algonquin Manuscript' at the Gilcrease Museum: An Anonymous Plagiarist of Gabriel Sagard," *Findings/Trouvailles*, April 30, 2018, https://champlainsociety. utpjournals.press/findings-trouvailles/2018/04/the-algonquin-manuscript-at-the-gilcrease-museum.

50. Wendy Stueck and Caroline Alphonso, "Changing History," *The Globe and Mail*, September 3, 2017, https://www.theglobeandmail.com/news/national/education/history-canada-indigenous-education/article36157403.

In a shortened note

> 51. Sayre, "The 'Algonquin Manuscript' at the Gilcrease Museum."
> 52. Stueck and Alphonso, "Changing History."

In a bibliography

> Sayre, Gordon M. "The 'Algonquin Manuscript' at the Gilcrease Museum: An Anonymous Plagiarist of Gabriel Sagard." *Findings/Trouvailles*, April 30, 2018. https://champlainsociety. utpjournals.press/findings-trouvailles/2018/04/the-algonquin-manuscript-at-the-gilcrease-museum.
>
> Stueck, Wendy and Caroline Alphonso. "Changing History." *The Globe and Mail*, September 3, 2017. https://www.theglobeandmail.com/news/national/education/history-canada-indigenous-education/article36157403.

A book review

In a note

> 53. Michael Bliss, review of *Sick Kids: The History of the Hospital for Sick Children*, by David Wright, with a forward by Mary Jo Haddad, *Canadian Historical Review* 98, no. 2 (June 2017): 403–5.
>
> 54. Steven Merritt Miner, "The Other Killing Machine," review of *Gulag: A History*, by Anne Applebaum, *New York Times*, May 11, 2003.

In a shortened note

> 55. Bliss, review of *Sick Kids*, 403.
> 56. Miner, "The Other Killing Machine."

In a bibliography

> Bliss, Michael. Review of *Sick Kids: The History of the Hospital for Sick Children*, by David Wright, with a forward by Mary Jo Haddad. *Canadian Historical Review* 98, no. 2 (June 2017): 403–5.

Miner, Steven Merritt. "The Other Killing Machine." Review of *Gulag: A History*, by Anne Applebaum, *New York Times*, May 11, 2003.

Video and audio
In a note

57. *Black Robe*, directed by Bruce Beresford (Montreal: Alliance Atlantis, 1991).

58. Ludwig van Beethoven, *Symphony No. 3, "Eroica,"* New York Philharmonic Orchestra, conducted by Leonard Bernstein, recorded 1964, Sony Classical, 1998, Naxos Music Library.

In a shortened note

59. *Black Robe*, directed by Bruce Beresford.

60. Beethoven, *Symphony No. 3*.

In a bibliography

Beethoven, Ludwig van. *Symphony No. 3, "Eroica."* New York Philharmonic Orchestra, conducted by Leonard Bernstein, recorded 1964. Sony Classical, 1998. Naxos Music Library.

Beresford, Bruce, dir. *Black Robe*. Montreal: Alliance Atlantic, 1991.

Archival materials
Every archive is organized differently, so the precise form of citations for archival materials will change depending on the materials. The most important consideration is to provide all the information necessary for a reader to trace your source. If you are conducting research in an archive, ask the archival staff if there is a correct way to cite their sources. Also be sure to spell out any abbreviations the first time you use them.

Citing a quotation of a quotation
Historians like to quote from original sources. If you see a primary source quotation in a secondary source and you want to quote it,

track down the primary source whenever possible and assess the accuracy of the quotation yourself. When you read the primary source, this entitles you to cite it directly. If you are not able to read the original—if it is kept in a distant archive that you cannot access, for example, or written in a language that you cannot read—then acknowledge the primary source in your citation, but say "as cited in" or "as quoted by" the secondary source.

Imagine that you are researching the importance of reputation in sixteenth-century Scotland, and you come across Elizabeth Ewan's essay "'Tongue You Lied': The Role of the Tongue in Rituals of Public Penance in Late Medieval Scotland." One particular quotation catches your eye, in which a man who had insulted his town's magistrates in 1552 was ordered to seek forgiveness of them and also to stop his tongue from insulting again. In the words of the original source, he was told to "refrane his twng fra sic sayingis in tyme cumming." When you check the endnote attached to this passage, you find that it is taken from "Dundee, Dundee Burgh Court, 3:186v." In the bibliography, you discover that this is a volume from the Dundee Burgh Court, an unpublished document in the Dundee City Archives in Scotland. You would like to use the colourful quotation in your own work, but cannot get to Dundee to consult the original. You can still use the quotation, but you have to provide a proper attribution.

In a note

61. Dundee City Archives, Book of the Church, Dundee Burgh Court Books 3: 186v, as cited in Elizabeth Ewan, "'Tongue You Lied': The Role of the Tongue in Rituals of Public Penance in Late Medieval Scotland," in *The Hands of the Tongue: Essays on Deviant Speech*, edited by E.D. Craun (Kalamazoo: Medieval Institute Publications, 2007), 123.

In a shortened note:

62. Dundee Burgh Court 3:186v, in Ewan, "Tongue You Lied," 123.

In a bibliography:

Ewan, Elizabeth. "'Tongue You Lied': The Role of the Tongue in Rituals of Public Penance in Late Medieval Scotland." In *The Hands of the Tongue: Essays on Deviant Speech*, edited by E.D. Craun, 115–36. Kalamazoo: Medieval Institute Publications, 2007.

Appendix C

Suggested Resources for Research and Writing in History

It would be impossible to list all the books, journals, and websites that could be of interest to history students, so this is just a small representative sample designed to give you a few starting points for what you might find helpful in your research and writing.

Professors often list recommended resources among their course materials. Check the syllabus and assignment sheets for suggestions, and consider speaking with your professor for additional ideas.

When doing a general online search, look for the websites of museums, art galleries, libraries, archives, universities in general, and history departments in particular. Be cautious of sites that include a lot of third-party advertising or other commercial material.

Some of the sites listed below are available only by subscription, which means that you will have access to the contents only if you have purchased a personal subscription or if your university, college, or local public library has purchased an institutional subscription. If you are having difficulty accessing the materials either directly through the main site or through your library catalogue, speak with a librarian.

Primary Sources

Library Guides
Your institution's library site may offer suggested resources for history students generally, or even for history students in specific courses or fields (such as Canadian history, East Asian history, the history of science, etc.). If your librarians have complied any LibGuides (content management systems for specific subjects, topics, or courses), make sure to consult these as well.

The University of Toronto Libraries' page on "Primary Source Databases for Historical Research," for example, offers links to primary source collections under a variety of headings, including "Major Collections," "Canada, U.S., Latin America," and "Africa & Middle East."

https://guides.library.utoronto.ca/primary

National and Local Archives

National and local archives in many countries are making their collections available online. For example, the Libraries and Archives Canada online collection contains a wide range of different sources, including films, newspapers, and government records. The Library and Archives Canada website provides several ways to search digitized archival material. The process can be a bit complex, so you should spend some time reading the finding aids to learn how to perform an effective search.
http://www.bac-lac.gc.ca/eng/Pages/home.aspx

World Digital Library

The World Digital Library contains significant historical documents from around the world and in more than one hundred languages. Primary source materials include government documents, maps, newspapers, prints, sound recordings, and film.
https://www.wdl.org/en

The Library of Congress Digital Collections

The Library of Congress has digitized its primary source holdings since 1994, providing digital access to collections that are unavailable anywhere else. The digital collection contains a wide range of primary source material primarily related to American history.
https://www.loc.gov/collections

Canadiana

Canadiana is a non-profit organization devoted to preserving Canada's heritage and making it accessible. Its collection includes the Early Canadiana Online virtual library, which holds many full-text primary source documents.
http://www.canadiana.org

The Internet History Sourcebooks Project

The Internet History Sourcebooks Project from Fordham University is a gateway to a rich set of collections of primary documents. They are arranged into separate sourcebooks on

topics such as ancient, modern, Islamic, women, African, gay and lesbian, and more.
https://sourcebooks.fordham.edu

Perseus Digital Library
The Perseus Digital Library was developed by Tufts University in 1987 and contains a large collection of primary and secondary sources for the study of ancient Greece and Rome, including English translations of ancient authors.
http://www.perseus.tufts.edu/hopper

Secondary Sources

Cambridge Histories
This reference collection from Cambridge University Press is an extremely useful resource for both background information and more detailed studies in a variety of fields. It currently has about 350 volumes in 10 subject areas: American History, Ancient History and Classical Studies, Asian History, British and European History, Global History, Literature, Middle East and African Studies, Music and Theatre, Philosophy and Political Thought, and Religion.

The Internet Public Library
The Internet Public Library is maintained mostly by volunteers from Drexel University in Philadelphia. Among its most useful links for historians are links to public libraries all over North America, a link to the Canadian literature archive, and a link on the homepage taking you to newspapers and magazines from all over the world.
http://www.ipl.org

Databases

Oxford Bibliographies Online
Oxford Bibliographies are authoritative research guides to scholarship in subjects across the humanities and social sciences.

Of particular interest to historians are their bibliographies in African American Studies, African Studies, Childhood Studies, Chinese Studies, Classics, Islamic Studies, Jewish Studies, Latin American Studies, Medieval Studies, Military History, and Renaissance and Reformation.

http://www.oxfordbibliographiesonline.com

JSTOR, Historical Abstracts, and Project MUSE

Large databases like JSTOR, Historical Abstracts, and Project MUSE can connect you to publications from a wide variety of publishers. It is worth investing some time in learning how to perform searches in them effectively so that you can make the most of their strengths.

https://www.jstor.org;   https://www.ebsco.com;   https://muse.jhu.edu

Music and Art

Oxford Music Online

Oxford Music Online provides access to authoritative reference works such as the *Oxford Dictionary of Music,* the *Oxford Companion to Music,* and *Grove Music Online.*

http://www.oxfordmusiconline.com

Oxford Art Online

Oxford Art Online provides access to authoritative reference works such as the *Oxford Companion to Western Art,* the *Benezit Dictionary of Artists,* and the *Grove Dictionary of Art.*

http://www.oxfordartonline.com

The Naxos Music Library

The Naxos Music Library contains more than 2 million tracks from over 800 recording labels. It is especially strong for Western classical music.

https://www.naxosmusiclibrary.com

Professional Historical Organizations and Institutions

The World History Association
The website of the World History Association includes links to the *Journal of World History* and other publications in the field of world history.
https://www.thewha.org

Canada's Virtual Museum
Canada's Virtual Museum site provides links to several thousand museums and heritage organizations.
http://www.virtualmuseum.ca

The British Museum
The British museum online collection contains over 4 million objects from around the world, including both ancient and modern artifacts.
http://www.britishmuseum.org

The Louvre
The Louvre makes available images of paintings, drawings, prints, and sculptures in the museum's collection.
https://www.louvre.fr/en

The Metropolitan Museum of Art
The Metropolitan Museum of Art makes available more than 375,000 images of artwork in the museum's collection. The collection contains artwork spanning 5000 years from across the world.
https://www.metmuseum.org

Writing Guides

The Chicago Manual of Style
Below is a link to the online version of *The Chicago Manual of Style*, the standard source for how to reference in history papers.
https://www.chicagomanualofstyle.org

Other standard guides that you may want to read cover-to-cover, or consult when necessary, include the following:

- Margery Fee and Janice McAlpine, *Guide to Canadian English Usage*, Second Edition (Oxford: Oxford University Press, 2011).
- H.W. Fowler, *Fowler's Dictionary of Modern English Usage*, edited by Jeremy Butterfield, Fourth Edition (Oxford: Oxford University Press, 2015).
- William Strunk, Jr., and E.B. White, *The Elements of Style*. There are many editions; choose a recent one.

The Oxford English Dictionary Online

The *Oxford English Dictionary Online* is a definitive guide to the meaning, history, and pronunciation of English words. Its entries are especially useful to historians because they provide information on how meanings of words have changed over time. http://www.oed.com

Glossary

The numbers in parentheses refer to the pages where the terms are first used. All terms are defined here as they are used in this book.

active voice (107) In a sentence using the active voice, the subject performs the action expressed by the verb.

anachronism (65) An anachronism occurs when something is misplaced out of its proper time.

analytical essay (69) An essay that examines an analytical problem (e.g., the relationship between science and culture). An analytical essay uses short narratives to shed light on the concept or problem under examination.

annotated bibliography (19) A list of sources that includes not only the publishing information of a typical bibliography, but also a brief description and assessment of each work.

archival material (10) Historical material, typically artifacts and primary documents, stored in archives.

argument (17) A claim in an essay that is supported by evidence and reason.

bibliography (4) A list of all the books, articles, documents, and other sources used in research. All the relevant publishing information, including author (and/or editor),

title, place and date of publication, and publisher, must be included.

block quotation (42) A quotation that is longer than three lines, set off from the main text in its own indented block, without quotation marks.

catalogue (6) A library's catalogue is the list of its holdings. It can usually be searched by author, title, or keywords.

citation (23) A reference note. Most citations include a specific page reference.

citation system (50) The particular system used to cite sources in a given work. Historians typically use the Chicago system (named after *The Chicago Manual of Style*) based on footnotes (or endnotes) and bibliographies. Other citation systems include MLA and APA, both of which use parenthetical referencing within the text.

cliché (121) A trite, overused phrase; for example, "in the nick of time."

colloquial language (119) Informal or casual language, including slang and contractions like "it's" that are not appropriate for formal history papers.

counterargument (34) An argument that challenges or potentially puts into question the main argument of an essay.

database (8) An online collection of materials such as documents or journal articles that are useful in specific fields of study. Often available only through library subscription.

deduction (63) Deductive reasoning reaches reasonable conclusions based on sometimes limited evidence; the most likely explanation.

draft (33) An early version of a piece of writing. For an essay, you should expect to write two or three drafts.

ellipses (43) Three dots (. . .) inserted into a quotation to show where words have been omitted. When using ellipses, remain true to the meaning of the original.

endnote (51) See **footnote**.

euphemism (120) An evasive word or phrase used to soften the message or avoid giving offence; for example, "vertically challenged" used in place of "short."

footnote (6) A reference note (flagged by a superscript number in the text) that identifies the source(s) on which a particular passage is based. Footnotes appear at the bottom of the relevant text pages; endnotes appear on separate pages at the end of the text. Most word-processing programs will create either form automatically.

historiography (ix) The study of the writing of history; the study of the discipline itself.

hypothesis (17) The proposition that drives research on a specific topic. It is tentative and subject to change after further investigation.

induction (63) Inductive reasoning reaches generalized conclusions after assembling many pieces of evidence.

inference (53) A conclusion based on the examination of evidence.

jargon (118) Technical or specialized words or phrases; generally inappropriate for use outside specific professions or groups.

narrative essay (74) An essay that may include analytical points but focuses on telling a single chronological story and generally arrives at one major conclusion.

outline (70) A way to show the general structure and most significant points of an essay. Often used as a stage in the writing process.

paraphrase (39) A rewording of a source's statement in roughly the same number of words (a shorter rewording is a summary).

passive voice (106) In a sentence using the passive voice, the subject receives the action expressed by the verb.

peer reviewer (13) A professional in the field who reviews the pre-publication text of a book or article to assess its accuracy and credibility and make recommendations for revisions. Articles published in scholarly journals are generally peer-reviewed by one or more reviewers. Some journals call this "refereed."

plagiarism (48) The use of someone else's words or ideas without proper acknowledgement.

primary source (3) A source written or created in the time period and at the place under study; a first-hand account.

proofreading (134) The reading of a text to find and correct any errors. Proofreading should take place at the very end of the revising and editing process.

secondary source (23) Typically, a book or article based on primary sources. The works written by historians are generally secondary sources, because they draw upon primary sources to reflect on earlier events.

summary (39) A concise restatement of a source's discussion, argument, etc.

superscript number (151) A small number written or printed above the line of text and used for referencing purposes. Each number corresponds to a footnote or endnote in which the author lists all the relevant publication and other information as necessary. Most word-processing programs today have automatic footnote or endnote functions, usually accessed through "references."

thesis (34) The central argument that a piece of historical writing sets out to maintain or prove; usually introduced early in the work in a "thesis statement."

transition sentence (83) A sentence that connects one part of an essay with another; typically used to end one paragraph or begin the next.

Index

FEEL ALIVE

RALPH SMART

FEEL ALIVE

FEEL ALIVE

RALPH SMART

INFINITE WATERS PUBLISHING INC

LONDON

Contents

Acknowledgements

This book is dedicated to all the wonderful free spirits around the world, those who dance in beauty and joy at the new world. A special thanks to my wonderful mother, beautiful sister, and my beloved partner. Every moment writing this book has been enjoyed. Life reveals itself more and more, as I dive deep within the depths of my soul. Sharing with the world frees my heart, and I will not stop doing so. Connecting with beautiful kindred spirits on the 'Infinite Waters Youtube Channel' is awesome—you are all appreciated and loved.

'Feel alive' is looking at aspects of life which affect us all: relationships, universal mind control, judgement, depression, fun, fear and love. The books finds solutions to live in harmony with the universe and to remember our true worth. The time has come on the planet to live free and in abundance. Many of us live, but how many feel alive?

To feel alive we must dive into the moment and remember we live in a flash of light. We are infinite beings who transcend time and space; as nature inspires me, I hope this book inspires you to become the best version of yourself.

The power lies within you. A big thanks to the universal energy permeating all existence—we are made from the same fabric...now is always.

Infinite love and balance to Everyone...Forever Free.

Chapter One

How to Clear Your Mind

"We live in the world we think of"

Breathe easy...just be. How do we live from our hearts? How do we free ourselves? On my journey I have realised the human mind is similar to a computer. In a computer you put programs, the more programs you put on a computer, the more it slows down, until it eventually crashes. The more we accumulate in the mind, the more we slow down, until we too eventually crash. Belief is the program that creates our reality, it's all BS—belief systems.

Whatever we are thinking, we are creating, in essence, we live in the world we are thinking of. Many of us want our minds instantly to switch off...that's impossible. The more effort you use to get into the effortless state, the harder it becomes. By surrendering, our heart space opens. Letting go off society's expectations, of what friends and family think, liberates you.

Accepting yourself 100% is the first step of clearing your mind and watching it dissolve. When we look at the world we live in, we do not know how it operates. The hidden mysteries of the world are a reflection of what's happening within ourselves. Everything we accept as real, has been put there as a program, this is what fills the mind. There are hundreds of thousands of these little programs filling the mind, just like a computer. To clear the mind we have to begin deleting each one, one by one.

"Can we look at people without judgement?"

Many of us look at people and see their race, colour, and nationality... all of this creates a tremendous amount of blockage within the mind. As children we are living free, we are living in the present moment, hence we are super powerful. Keeping alive the inner child in you is essential to clear your mind. Many of our parents took us out of the present moment. The first time they asked you:

"What do you want to be when you grow up?"

The spell was cast. Now we are thinking in the future;

"I want to be a lawyer."

We are projecting into the future which has not even taken place yet. There is no need to worry over something you do not have control over.

Assumptions make bad conclusions, you feel you know people, you do not. Honesty is key to clearing the mind, we need a reality check—the human being is on the run from itself. Many of us live as prisoners in our own minds. Moving from doing to being is essential to tap into the flow, this is where source energy lives. Animals live in the flow, they are free to be, free to enjoy life.

There are only two forces in the universe, love and fear. Many of us are running around like headless chickens, therefore we are caught in perpetual fear, and distraction. On the planet, silence is feared. The void is the 'existential vacuum,' the emptiness where you find your true power. Embracing the silence helps you clear your mind.

The internal dialogue, the voices in our heads. "I'm not good enough," this negative self talk fills the minds of many. When we can transcend the negative and the positive, we begin to clear our minds. By seeing the world in duality, divided, and fragmented...this is what we become. The external is a reflection of what's taking place within us. 不二.

Embrace the positive and negative self talk, then the mind will not be able to tell the difference and will not disturb you. The biorhythms of many of us are out of sync. The new paradigm is about tuning into ourselves, that's another way to clear the mind.

"Do the foods we eat promote our wellness? Are we eating sun foods or plant based foods?"

All of this affects our minds on a molecular level. We have to eat foods which raise our vibration higher. Many of us living in a low vibration, suffer from a confused mind, the mind becomes cloudy and dull. Once you have lost the spark of life it's over. To reignite the flame we have to begin deleting old programs. We have to let go of everything we think we know about life.

Many of us are born into a religion, when we remember we are made from the same fabric as the universe, there is no external messiah coming to save you. We are what we seek. All of this frees your mind because the search is over. Many of us are on the quest for enlightenment, enlightenment is knowing how much you do not know. This clears your mind, as you see you are living in a world of infinite possibilities.

The new paradigm is where people of the world connect with fellow kindred spirits, to create a whole new world. Clearing your mind is living from your heart. To live from your heart you have to step outside of linear time which is man-made. 十三月を下.

There is enough to go around on the planet. We have been lured into a false sense of security. Security is what many desire, the job that pays a certain amount at the end of the week. This security is what enslaves us. To clear your mind you have to let go of your security. When something is secure what happens? It cannot move. In these cities we have secure jobs, but we cannot move, to clear your mind you must become fluid like the ocean. The power lies within.

We are under a big spell, it's frightening, the more you delve deeper, the more you see how universal mind control has taken its toll. There is a war for the hearts and minds of the people, whoever can enter your mind first—wins. To clear our minds we have to break the spell from within, we have to take back our power. Money is a spell, race is a spell, religion is a spell, to be a sovereign being we must let all of that go—let go of the illusion, embrace nature.

Walking around barefoot in the soil can help clear our minds. Many of us are wearing trainers and shoes, "How can we feel anything?" We are concealed in what we wear, therefore we are concealed in how we think... our spirit is concealed, we do not even know it. The more you begin to take off the layers, the more you begin to clear your mind. Stripping everything bare to its original organic essence is the way to be free. We have been played on the planet, but what goes around comes around. How we treat other life forms on the planet is how we are being treated.

When we begin to look at animals with respect and not butcher them, then maybe things will change. On an energetic level, when we butcher animals their energy is being passed on to us. Information is stored in water, Dr Emoto's research shows this, therefore blood contains water. The animals information is being passed into millions of people around the globe, they are taking on this fear and agony—this is what we are creating on a mass scale.

The world is changing as more people become aware, we are not the only superior life form on the planet. Every life form deserves the same treatment—respect. People are getting the wakeup call, this is the information age...the hidden is coming to light. The veil is being lifted, the word 'apocalypse' means removing the veil, all of this will help clear the mind. Do not fear the unknown, many of us want to stay in our comfort zone because it's safe—if you do not venture out, you will never clear your mind, because you will always be wondering what is on the other side. Giving yourself your own unique value system is a great way to clear the mind, do not let anybody give you value—love yourself 100%.

Chapter Two

How to Raise Your Frequency
"There is only now."

Many of us on our journeys come to the cross roads, feeling stuck and dense. One of the quickest ways to raise your vibration is to have as much fun as possible. When we go back to our childhood, we were always having fun, because we lived in the present. There was no fear—fear only exists in the future. There is a huge shift happening on Earth—a global awakening. No matter where you are, so many feel their whole life in a blink of an eye is changing.

Why should it matter about raising the frequency? Within us exists two natures, higher and lower nature, we need both of these parts. To exist only in your lower nature is what's happened to many of us, however merging with your higher nature taps us into our true authenticity. Children enter this dimension magnificent, somewhere along the line, we become stuck, we slow down, and our vibration decreases. Terminally ill patients have a slow vibration because their life force is withering.

Being happy increases your vibration, it's not what you do, it's how you feel when you are doing it. To raise the frequency, eat foods which nourish you, not because they taste good, but because they fortify you with supreme strength. Having a healthy relationship with food will make you glow. On my journey once I let go of heavy foods (fast foods), a healing miracle within happened.

Food is information from the cosmos, Mother Earth is providing all the information inside food. Organic foods give us life, and boosts our energy. Much of the food on the planet is drug food, this robs our energy. Natural foods contain enzymes to digest foods, junk foods have no enzymes to digest food, therefore they have to steal healthy cells inside your body to help with the digestion process. Grapes, avocados, kale, are some of the living foods which will raise your vibration.

"How do you know when your vibration is raised?"

I had this euphoria along my journey—I stopped judging others. To live in non judgement is the only way to be free, not judging people will help raise your vibration. A lot of times we see people and ask:

"How old are you? Where were you born?"

This is normal, however analysing every detail in others will only separate you, which is the—grand illusion. Analysis is paralysis, it takes us out of the present moment, where we lose power.

Children fly high, there is no time to say:

"I do not like your skin colour."

We are wondering about the differences on planet Earth, wait until we go beyond this universe, there are many life forms waiting for us.

"Why do we worry about petty things?"

When you allow yourself the time to be yourself this increases your vibration...you tap into your authenticity.

We wear masks day to day, a different mask for your family, friends, and work colleagues. Nobody knows who you are, you do not even know yourself. In my early journey I was going through life like a loose leaf of a branch. Connecting back to source empowers you. To raise our vibration, we must not externalise power. We are made from the same fabric cloth as the universe, therefore in honouring myself—I honour everything in existence.

Many people around the globe are worshipping outside of themselves...this slows down your frequency, because you are moving away from source...which is you. We are an extension of source energy, once we deviant from source, it becomes cold...icy. We feel like our life is falling into pieces. We live in the age of manipulation, great distractions, however once you go within you see your infinite power.

Heaven is a state of mind, there is no heaven or hell—there is only what you create at this present moment. The angels and demons are archetypes of yourself. We are everything in existence. Connecting with kindred spirits will raise your vibration, being in the presence of luminous souls. We attract what we are. Some people say:

"I do not trust anybody," well you will continue to meet people you cannot trust.

When we let go of self limiting belief systems, it frees us. Many have a 'Yolo' attitude on the planet—you only live once. Let's not follow nature, if that's how you want to live...fine. Cutting ourselves from the infinite possibilities that could potentially exist, diminishes our growth—life is the eternal mystery. Life is the unknown which is constantly revealing itself to us.

Awakening to a world of infinite possibilities shows us another way.

"What kind of music is going out to the masses?"

Sound can help raise your vibration. Playing an instrument is a wonderful way to heal yourself. Dr Emoto has shown how sound interacts with water, the way we talk, everything is connected. Let go of fear—false evidence appearing real. Fear is a self created feeling, based on a pseudo realisation we do not have the capacity to overcome a perceived experience. Everything is based on the perception we have of ourselves.

To have the best perception of ourselves, we must let go of who we think we are. I am not a name, nation, job, religion, or democrat—I am. What we see of people is a tiny side of their true selves. We are multi-dimensional beings having a human experience. There is only now, tune into the moment, and do what you have always dreamed. Aligning with your inner truth makes you—powerful beyond measure.

Chapter Three

5 Ways to Relieve Panic
"Smile more."

These are some tools which have helped on my journey to relieve panic, stress and anxiety:

1. Bring emotions into the present.
The 'Freeze' is where many of us standstill in the past or future, we must experience the 'now' to access our true power. Clapping when you have 'The Freeze' moment will help you enter the present moment. Body awareness is essential for dealing with panic, many of us our out of tune with ourselves, we do not know when we are anxious. To free yourself from panic, realise the body is the unconscious mind. The body, mind, and spirit are interconnected and interchangeable.

When you feel your body becoming tense, breathe deeply. Breathing deeply improves the blood circulation around the body, you bring inner calmness and balance.

"How do you feel at the present moment?"

Many of us are anxious because we are thinking in the past or future. Become present to your body, ask yourself:

"How do I feel?""

Automatically your body relaxes. Feeling tense is a choice—tense mind equals tense body and spirit.

2. Own your emotions and take responsibility.
We must be responsible for how we feel. Seeing we have no control of what others think or feel, we must let go of attempting to change

others perceptions of ourselves. The perception of ourselves is the only thing that matters.

"How do you see yourself?"

Remembering we are creating our own reality based on thoughts and feelings, helps us take responsibility for where we find ourselves. It's easy to blame others for our panic. How we respond to others is key in letting go of anxiety.

3. Changing your focus.
   "Do you focus on what you want or what you fear?"

Visualising where you want to be will alleviate your anxiety, when you let go...snap out of it. Many people are caught in drama, so this is what creates our reality. To free your heart, it's essential to release the panic, but first our minds must be free.

Thinking outside of the box, not thinking in a linear way, not closing ourselves to others, all helps to relieve panic. By opening up yourself to the world, smiling more—the panic disappears.

4. Change your lifestyle and know thyself.
   Ask yourself:

"What am I doing to promote wellness in my life? Are you in the right environment?"

By taking a simple walk through nature, your mind clears. Do not go where the crowd is all the time, take time to be alone and connect with your true self. The environment is everything. To know thyself, we have to ask ourselves what does our soul resonate with?

"What brings you happiness or joy? Are you doing that? Are you living the life you want to live?"

Many of us are caught in panic, because we are not doing what we love to do. Exercising helps release the powerful endorphins, making us feel better and calmer. The relationship we have with time must change, if we are to be panic free. Nowadays I do not wear a watch, because I see we are limitless beings who are timeless. Many of us are time slaves...the power lies within your hands—will you take back your power?

The lifestyles many live make us feel inadequate. Right now on the planet it's time for elevation, time to reclaim our power. Much of the fears we have, emanate from externalising power...giving it away. To access our true power we must go on the inward journey and take our place in the universe once again.

The lifestyle we live, includes the foods we consume, you are what you eat, drink and think. Ask yourself:

"What am I putting into my body? Do I feel calmer or more tense?"

Live raw plant based foods have a soothing energy on your body; nervousness decreases, once we let go of junk foods.

Feel liberated by simply changing your diet.

"Are you creating enough time for yourself? Are you loving yourself?"

Many do not love themselves enough, we are caught in looking for the validation from someone or something external to us. When you give yourself value, it does not matter how much money you make, you feel at peace.

"Are you doing what you are passionate about?"

"Do you love the image you have of yourself? This is essential when letting go of panic.

Have fun, celebrate, enjoy life to the fullest, because you are worthy. Knowing you are worthy, frees your spirit from the chains of fear. Having a lighter heart requires letting go of toxic energy, always purifying yourself.

Let go of all that holds you back; the memories, events, people, anything that makes you feel worse, leave it at the door, and walk outside of the house.

"How much are you carrying?"

Becoming lighter is the only way to fly, this is the only way to relieve panic.

5. Stop competing and comparing yourself with others. Everybody you see is living their own unique journey, you do not have to fight or survive for your piece of cake. *

Everyone is unique...I am another yourself in a different time and space. When you stop competing, you fall into your own niche and panic fades away...you do not have to win.

Running up against someone else is an illusion, there is enough for everyone. Looking at the world in abundance, diminishes anxiety, and allows you to breathe. Everyone is here for a different reason, but find your true gift and transform your world. We are here to have the most beautiful time on planet Earth—let's have fun. //.

* There is enough space for everybody so that we can joyfully express our unique creativity.

Chapter Four

Love Yourself 100%

"Where do you feel most free...Go there."

2022.05.03

00:25
=>

The new paradigm is about seeing your true worth as an infinite being, to live the most awesome human experience. To love yourself, you must keep alive and tap into your inner child.

"Where do you feel most free?"

Go there, within that special place, you will find your true power.

Many of us are not happy where we are, but fail to see we are creating our own reality through choices and thoughts.

The power lies within us. Loving yourself opens you up to others and expands your heart space. Before you can love anybody, you have to love yourself. The notion of 'Love Thy Neighbour' has become popular on the planet, this is all well and good, but many people suffer from a low self esteem.

Low confidence levels emanate from the validation from someone else, the waiting for approval. Letting go of society's expectations is the greatest way to begin to love yourself. Throw away the TV as far as you can. Much of our ideas about the world come from the television, who controls your perception, controls your reality. Once you begin to love yourself you see how subliminal manipulation is used in every area of our society. Someone is advertising this product to become happy, no, self love begins internally first. Nobody can give you anything you do not already have.

All your experiences are coming deep within yourself, it's all you. Loving yourself is not about being a narcissist, it's when we tap into our true self. We can only do this when we give ourselves time and are not so hard on ourselves.

Letting go of this idea of perfection is a great way to love yourself 100%. Many people we view as beautiful may not feel beautiful inside; it takes changing our perception to love ourselves 100%.

Seeing yourself as a unique sovereign being, who came to this planet to be a powerful co-creator, generates the self love energy. Since we are made from the same fabric as the universe, we are not here to worship externally. We are here to serve and exchange with one another...not one single deity or job.

In loving yourself you have to take responsibility where you find yourself. The body is a vehicle, we are in the driving seat. Amazing things happen when you love yourself. Accept your flaws are not flaws. they are hidden aspects of yourself. Many of us do not want to enter the 'shadow land'—we are afraid to see the deep dark aspects of ourselves.

The darkness is equally as important as the light. In our darkest moments we become illuminated, that's what it takes to love yourself. We must go into the deep depths of our souls to find the pearls that lie within.

The time has come to love yourself; stop competing with others, this takes you out of your element. Be happy, content and fulfilled with yourself, because we are where we choose to be.

"Why desire to be someone else?"

When you love yourself 100%, you see yourself as an artist, you appreciate everyone's unique gift. There is nobody like you, so why are you worried about someone taking your place?

Many do not love themselves, they say if only I become someone else, everything will be perfect. We can never become another, all we can do is accept ourselves 100% and start—loving ourselves. 00:3

Chapter Five

Why Am I Single?
"You cannot force love."

O n my journey I used to ask this question, however, I realised something was missing in my life. Nobody was to blame, it was the relationship I had with myself. Sexual energy is the energy that permeates everything in existence, in essence, sexual energy is creative energy. Many of us on the planet are wondering where our beloved is, if you wonder why you have not met the dream woman/man...don't worry—your time will come.

For so many of us we want a quick fix. The greatest relationship we can have is with ourselves. Through my metamorphosis, I saw you have to love yourself, before you can love anybody else. When you embrace your flaws, gifts, and talents, you begin to accept other people's flaws, gifts and talents—nobody is perfect. Perfectionism is a curse...although nature is a perfect.

There is no dream person, you have to take on board the good, bad, and the ugly. Many single people have a check list. Ultimately we are all looking for our reflection. We are looking for the other half of ourselves, which is in essence—our higher selves. Once you tap into your higher self, the marriage happens between yourself.

The union of the body and the mind, soul and spirit, this is the true marriage. Going to a temple or church does not make you married, true marriage is within yourself, then you meet someone else—then the two wholes become complete.

Many people around the world are fragmented within themselves, you cannot be half looking for another half...because now you have two incomplete halves. There are times, seasons, and cycles within the universe, it may not be tomorrow you may find your partner, but it will happen. We all should be sharing this life journey with someone we can help evolve and in return help us evolve—pushing us towards our greatest highest potential. We must merge with the greater part of ourselves.

Letting go of society's expectations; dates, and calendars is key to meeting your beloved. Instant Gratification has been the way of the world for so long:

"I want it now!"

Love does not work like that, forming deep relationships take a long time in terms of developing an inner intimate knowing. Developing a deeper intimacy and helping another person take of the mask, requires surrendering 100%. The more you tap into who you are and become whole, the more you will attract people to you—you will attract your reflection. We attract what we are...what we send out is what we attract.

Many women say all men are dogs, they only want sex:

"Guess what?"

These are the kinds of men they attract. By thinking like this, they are sending a signal to the universe—the infinite genie, and the universe will reply to you:

"Your wish is my command."

Once you open your heart to the universe to meet your reflection and let go...it manifests.

There are millions of single people around the world, this is not a bad thing. Sometimes it may be from choice, some take the time to find themselves and discover who they are. Going to the wilderness is best gone alone. Many people in relationships are not happy...they just don't want to be alone.

Some single people are using this time to reconnect back to their true inner power and develop their clarity and inner balance. This is in order for when they do meet that extraordinary person they fall in love with, they know instantly—because they have done the inner work.

Not doing the inner work can leave us single, once you work on yourself, you see you do not have to search. Along my journey I used to search, I got into a relationships with a sense of urgency. So many of us are afraid to lose the one we love, we can only lose what does not belong to us. I do not own anybody on the planet, we must allow others to become themselves.

In many of our relationships we feel certain people belong to us, that's why many relationships don't last in today's world—it's based on owner-ship. Being single can also be a fun experience. Many ancient masters possessed such a deep connection to their heart, they never needed a partner. They developed the true marriage, between the yin feminine essence and the yang masculine essence, which exists within all of us.

On Earth it's great to be in a loving relationship with someone to raise superhuman children. Being single should not worry us, do not be anxious, the more anxious you are, the more you deviate from your true authentic self. I would rather someone hate me for who I am, than to love me for who I am not.

There are lots of internet dating sites, I even went on a few, however when I let go of the search, everything manifested. Online dating is on the rise; with many hoping to land next to their dream partner. Once you clear your senses, when you see the one...you will know.

Single people must throw away the check list, life is dynamic, the only permanent being—change. Nobody is ever one thing, we only show others what we want them to see. Along my journey I told myself I am going to let go of finding the perfect person, instead I will work on myself and be open to a fellow kindred spirit..everything changed. Life is—forever changing.

Some people are in the most wonderful relationships...but it's just time to move on. Every single person we are in a relationship with, is a teacher. Some of us are recovering from horrendous relationships. Seeing that we attract relationships to us, allows us to take responsibility and—feel alive. Being single is a choice we all have, it's not negative or positive, it is whatever you make it.

There are beautiful people around the planet, asking:

"Where is my other half?"

Your other half is your higher self. Once you see your reflection in someone else, you connect with them, if your creation is no longer needed, you connect with someone else...you cannot force love.

Chapter Six

How to Deal With Universal Mind Control
"The power lies within."

Have you ever watched a TV program it was so hard to get up? Soaps, dramas, comedy shows, and sports keep us entertained. Along my journey I have seen how this is one big distraction. The whole world is waking up to see how we are addicted to so many things outside of ourselves. Everywhere you go, there seems to be some kind of distraction. An advert, billboard poster, newspaper, television show...it seems everyone is after your mind. We live in a society of instant gratification, quick fixes and—24/7 grinds.

To free your mind you must let go of society's expectations. Fitting in is not the solution, but rather, becoming yourself in a world attempting to change you every minute. There is a war for the hearts and minds of the people...it's all a test. Once we turn off the noise and distraction, we discover our true selves as brilliant luminous beings. The television...tells lies to your vision, we have to—tell our vision.

We waste endless hours watching other people's lives, but ask yourself:

"What are you doing with your life?"

Seeing your favourite football player scoring a goal can give many a euphoric feeling, however many live through these sports stars vicariously.

"Whose life are you more interested in, yours or someone else's?"

Other people's lives seem far more entertaining, glamorous, and glorious than ours.

Many of us on the planet have been asleep and we do not even want to find the alarm clock. Ignorance is bliss, just as long we are dancing or singing, we are happy. Ignorance is not bliss, many people are dying prematurely, their lives have been turned into a living hell...because they have no knowledge of self. What freed me on my journey was seeing we are living in an amusing park, a great show, however, realising you are the director...you reclaim your power.

A lot of people go to college or university, but they come out in huge debt—so they have to be working for the rest of their lives. This perpetual cycle is what's keeping humanity in a low vibration. A lot of people have masters and degrees, but are flipping burgers in Mcdonald's...what happened? We fail to see the greatest education we can have is becoming intimate with ourselves.

We live in a matrix game dream world, built around power and control. Fighting the external world will not change it...be the change you wish to see. What you fight you give power too, in essence, resistance makes stronger. Magic can only take place when you are not paying attention. The distraction works through separation...look at religion:

"My God is better than yours."

We must be free from all authority, including yourself.

Once you can be free of your own authority, you see enlightenment is knowing how much you do not know. The distraction is always to externalise your power. The distraction is always to be busy, we feel everything is happening so fast, but that's the trick.

Many of us are in a hurry to get nowhere fast. Harvesting cows for milk and chickens for eggs is a modern preoccpuation, however, we are also being harvested and manipulated on a grand level.

Being free of mind control is about delving into the hidden depths of your spirit, and entering the vast shadow land. When you do not follow the crowd, you go beyond the crowd—finding the pearls that lie within.

Once you see, you are not what society tells you, you tap into your infinite power.

To remember you cannot save everyone frees you, and you see we have to allow others the freedom of experiencing their own reality and truth. Embracing nature is one of the best ways, I have dealt with universal mind control. Plant your feet in Gaia and feel the orgasmic energy.

Letting go of stress by surrounding yourself with fellow kindred spirits carrying beautiful energies, helps clear our mind.

Eating fruits and sun foods which bring life into our body also helps us maintain balance, let go of fear and find your true power—The power lies within.

Chapter Seven

How to Deal With Difficult People?
"What you focus on grows."

How do you deal with people you can't stand? It may be your next door neighbour, friend, or even close family member. Throughout my journey, I have seen there are no positive people or negative people... there is only resonance. Five magnificent ways to deal with difficult people I use in my daily life are:

1. Do not take it personal.

A lot of people's problems are not our problems, they are theirs. You can't please everyone, if someone does not like you, that's too bad, all you can do is smile at them. Many people project personal issues onto you.

2. Stay calm.

How we feel internally is how we carry ourselves externally. Once you can smile, when you are dealing with someone you do not resonate with, you feel lighter and enter inner balance. Keep your head up while talking to people—remember your body is the unconscious mind.

Many people walk around their whole life with heads facing downwards towards the ground. Keeping straight bent backs...helps us stand our grand. Confronting people is not the answer, but do not suppress feelings...remember the power is within.

Breathing easy is essential, many difficult people want us to fall into their 'reaction tap.'

Whatever you fight you give energy too, therefore resistance makes stronger. Becoming silent within helps you develop inner strength, courage, and balance; the difficult person is no longer difficult. There are no difficult people, it's our interpretation of what is difficult. Everyone finds different people difficult. Everything in the universe is based on resonance, based on the law of affinity, therefore—we attract what we are.

3. Put things in perspective...stop worrying, start living.
"How important is this difficult person?"

To move past any difficult person or situation, you have to let go. We must change the way we react to people, before we change the way we interact with them. Everything is based on how we react, we have to take responsibility.

There is so much happening in the world;

"Why would you let someone's fear consume you?"

"How are you going to use your energy?"

The more you focus on something the more it grows, therefore— change your focus. Putting things in perspective helps you to fly beyond them. Ask yourself:

"How is this person holding up a mirror to me?"

Many people we call difficult, are in essence helping us discover our true selves. They are allowing us to see unresolved issues within ourselves. Taking responsibility for your own feelings and actions, ensures other people are no longer the cause.

4. Put yourself in their shoes.
We are all coming from different backgrounds; having empathy, which is the ability to recognise other people's emotions, frees you. Seeing where others are coming from, how they see the world, means you can rise above any situation.

Learning how to not take people so serious, you see this difficult person is no longer difficult—but a walk in the park.

5. Keep it moving.
Do not dwell on what difficult people have to say...in one ear, out the other. In life the universe gives everyone a job. These difficult people are needed on the planet, because they help you tap into your true self. Nature has a sense of humour and that's what we need when dealing with difficult people.

The more you think of other people who bring you down, the more you become them. When you smile the energy has to pass through you first, before it reaches the other person. The attitude we take is essential when dealing with difficult people...how we respond. We cannot control how other people act—only how we react.

We came to this planet to have the most expansive human experience possible and awaken to a world of infinite possibilities. There is no time for petty thoughts, you are worth more.

Every difficult person you meet is there as a teacher for you. Once you pass the test they are here to teach you, they no longer become difficult. They are difficult, because they are the test for you...your greatest adversary is your greatest friend.

Sticks and stones may break my bones, but words will never hurt me, words do hurt. Words are vibrations, we must not give other people's words, power over our internal condition. Remaining neutral is key, changing your internal environment to uplift your spirit and inner balance. Lots of us place ourselves in hostile environments, where there are lots of difficult people around.

Connect with kindred spirits, many difficult people take away our joy, but they are not negative—only...there is no resonance there. Every moment spent thinking over someone undesirable, you are taking away a moment of pure bliss—learn from the past, but don't live there.

The 'Emotional Drive By' is a term I coined regarding how other people dump their garbage onto you. They drive up, leave all their problems with you, then speed off in an abrupt hurry...be aware of the 'Emotional Drive By.' We have to purify our senses whilst dealing with difficult people; we came here to shine, let nobody take away your—glow.

Chapter Eight

The Wonders of Whole Foods
"You are what you eat....and feed your senses."

By changing your diet, it will change your lifestyle and outlook forever—boosting your energy. Today I have an appreciation for people in spite of what family and friends think, still persevere, and go with what their hearts tells them.

Food has been a major component along my journey of self healing. Natural foods, such as bananas, dates and mangoes, keep us more alive and awake. Eating less processed foods and more whole foods will restore the body's natural energy systems.

Whole foods are nature's natural original produce. They come with complete enzymes to help digest the food. Much of the food we eat in today's world is devoid of enzymes, hence we are stuck...constipated. The body has a question mark:

"How will I digest this food?"

Stealing from healthy cells is the only way the body can compensate and digest the food. Many young people eat candy and fast food, however remain glowing. One day, however. everything changes; when the body can longer replace healthy cells...then you begin to age. The bleaching of foods, for instance, brown bread into white, has made many people unwell on the planet.

Always go for the more organic as opposed to the more refined. Nature has blessed fruits, vegetables and grains with all the nutrients and minerals we need to thrive. Milk made from nuts such as cashew, has all the calcium the body needs. What the mass production of food has done is to strip foods of their nutrients, bleach them, refine them with sugars...

then fortify them with nutrients. Nature's food is perfect;

"So why change it?"

We think we can continue to overload the body with junk but it will catch up with us in the end. The liver does a great job cleansing the body, but it needs help from us putting in high vibration food. Get creative in the kitchen, mix different colours and flavours—have fun.

Avocados are my favourite fruit. Filled with vitamin E, and oleic acid, it contains carotenoid lutein which prevents against macular degeneration, caused from staring at computer screens too long.

There is a big myth surrounding food, this is the 'protein myth...' we worry about not getting enough. The reason why people eat meat they will tell you is because of protein.

"Protein, protein, protein..."

Many of the animals we kill for food, obtain protein from the grass, plants and vegetables. Water and air contain protein, nature is abundant and gives us everything we need. We cannot survive without air for more than a few minutes; it's the 'Chi' which keeps life flowing.

Eating whole foods have transformed my life in unimaginable ways. The majority of us are under a huge spell and programmed. Culture and tradition have enormous influences over our food choices.

I do not feel people who eat meat are different from those who do not, or vegans are more superior...all of these are labels...tags. Doing what resonates with your heart and soul is key—there are no merit points for anybody.

Not only does what we eat affect our wellness, also how we think and our attitude. We are what we feed all of our senses. There are some people on a plant based diet, but also give of a toxic energy through the words and actions they harbour. We have to become whole in all areas of life. Respecting all life forms has helped me on my journey. Animals were created for their own reasons not for our consumption.

We are not emotionally ready to kill our own food. There is a pattern within everything in nature, it's no surprise what we do to animals, we do onto ourselves, more so...the planet. We cannot kill in violence and expect peace on Earth. Seeing you can impact the ecosystem by living in harmony with the universe is liberating.

How we treat other animals is not a sign of an evolved species right now on the planet. We have so much work to do, to see animals have their own purpose. We are supposed to be helping animals not eating them. Everyone sees things in different ways...but awaken to your truth within.

We can all co-exist in harmony on the planet. I have friends and family who consume meat, and I love them nevertheless. Where you are in your own energetic vibration will dictate what foods you choose, and how you think and see the world.

Organic foods reveal the colours and patterns of life, it's about going back to nature, embracing it, and loving life. They reveal the interconnectedness between everything, and you feel lighter for it. The sun has cooked the food for us already, live foods contain all the nourishment and healing energies from the sun. Cooking food to death has become trendy, but nature has already cooked the food in its natural state. High temperature foods kills off enzymes inside the food, a gentle steaming who do less harm.

Look to consume foods as close to their original state as possible. Life is a wonderful journey...no matter where you go, you see—nature's infinite abundance.

Chapter Nine

Can Psychedelics Take You to Heaven?
"Heaven is a state of mind."

Heaven is a state of mind, not some place you go after you die, but a moment you create in the present. Many are searching for enlightenment or nirvana, I have come to see enlightenment is knowing how much you don't know. Many people are not happy with the state of the world and do not want to be here.

A psychedelic substance is a psychoactive drug whose primary action is to alter cognition and perception. The common psychedelics are LSD, Ayahuasca , Magic Mushrooms, and Salvia. Salvia is an Entheogen, used in Mexico for centuries to awaken and generate the power within. Entheogen, a term derived from the Greek 'entheos', directly translated to mean having "God (theos) within" or more loosely translated as "inspired" and 'genesthe' meaning "to generate".

'Entheos' was typically used to describe poets, musicians and other artists who were believed to receive their gifts from the divine. The word entheogen thus exposes itself as meaning "that which generates God/the divine in a person". The amazing herb Salvia was used to induce powerful visions for healing, and was also prescribed remedially for headaches and rheumatism.

Psychedelics have been known to create altered states of consciousness and unlock the hidden mysteries of the brain. In Ancient Egypt people took the blue lotus plant, Nymphaea Caerulea, its psychoactive properties are now being rediscovered. On the walls, Egyptian art shows members of society holding the blue lotus flower in reverence and praise. There is a possibility this flower may have given ancient Egyptians altered states of reality to create a world of infinite possibilities.

Cannabis and Marijuana are herbs which many use to 'feel high' and calm their senses. Cannabis is a leafy plant which grows wild in many of the tropic and temperate areas of the world. It is cultivated both indoors and out for the production of its flowering tops A compound found in cannabis could halt the spread of many forms of aggressive cancer, scientists say.

Researchers found that the compound, called cannabidiol, had the ability to 'switch off' the gene responsible for metastasis in an aggressive form of breast cancer. Importantly, this substance does not produce the psychoactive properties of the cannabis plant. The team from the California Pacific Medical Center, in San Francisco, first spotted its potential five years ago, after it stopped the proliferation of human breast cancer cells in the lab. A Harvard study also says Marijuana cures cancer.

Many herbs are still illegal despite the evidence they may have medical benefits. Many people have overdosed on LSD, this is why the drug has been banned in many parts of the world. The fear of psychedelics in the collective mind is prevalent, they are seen as something not to partake in...dangerous.

Many countries have banned all kinds of psychedelics altogether. On my journey I have seen that psychedelics and herbs are 'Earth enhancers' and have a great instrinsic healing power.

The human body is an amazing instrument, I see the power within us and once you 'know thyself,' you can create your own natural high. The brain is the largest pharmacy in the world, I know it can produce all the healing properties of the herbs people take.

We must activate our pineal glands to tap into our infinite reservoir of power. Many of us take herbs, but it can act as a crutch if we do not take responsibility for our own internal condition. Once you become dependent on external drugs, you face the possibility of deep addiction... living in fear if you are without them.

Living free as a sovereign being you see everything exists within yourself, we are plant, stars—the universe itself. Paying for herbs can also be an expensive affair, and many people live in debt because of it. We cannot be sure how pure the herbs we take are, if we are not picking them, there is a chance they could have been mixed with other harmful herbs...giving us unwanted symptoms.

Many have said there is a conspiracy why certain herbs are banned, because they do not want people to access their true power and enter other dimensions. Natural herbs found in mother nature are extraordinary, however you do not need them to get to heaven, after all, heaven is a state of mind—know thyself.

Chapter Ten

I Lost My Job, What Should I Do?

"Everyday is a new start."

Losing a job can be devastating, but we must never give up hope and see this as a great window of opportunity to follow our dreams. Depression and fear follow joblessness, therefore its essential to keep spirits high by any means necessary.

The jobs we have, give many people value, meaning and purpose in their lives. Once we lose our jobs, so many people feel undervalued and diminished...not where they belong. The panic alarm rings and fear begins to consume many people's hearts and minds. Feeling stuck not knowing what to do or where to turn, can make us feel alone.

Losing a job can feel like our world is coming to an abrupt end and the whole world is falling apart. We must remember the way out of the dark tunnel is to see the light at the end. Once we can let go of society's expectations, we begin to free ourselves.

Creating your own unique value system is the first step to overcoming job loss, and getting rid of depression. Giving yourself your own unique definition is a great way to not allow anybody to place value over you.

Many on the planet suffer from an 'identity crisis,' the jobs we have give us an identity, without them we feel—empty. Letting go of 'status anxiety' is a great way to be when dealing with unemployment.

Many people lose jobs and feel loneliness, therefore connecting to a community, or spiritual source is essential to give your life purpose. When you lose your job you find your work. We are living in a sea of infinite potentials, a world where anything is possible. Everything is based on belief, how you think affects how you feel. This may be the most rewarding time of your life, grab this opportunity to experience life to the max.

Catch up with old friends, go out, have fun, or why not take that holiday you have always dreamed of. Let go of guilt, if you have just lost a job, see you can always find another one.

By cultivating talents and gifts you will always have a job. What you can offer to society depends how you cultivate your gifts. Embrace your passion and do what you love in this period and recognise you can create your own job.

Working a 9-5 job is not for everyone, there are other options such as becoming your own boss. This will take self discipline, waking up early is essential for getting the most out of yourself whilst you have not got a job. Feel better by having a similar wake up routine as you had in your previous job. Also physical exercise will boost your spirits by releasing powerful endorphins to make you feel alive once again.

Be thankful your alive and count your many blessings, remember you have your health, you have life. Appreciating this as a wondrous opportunity will help you put life in perspective, which is key to not 'going off the rails.'

Love yourself 100% and see that you are a marvellous brilliant luminous being—losing a job cannot take that from you. Search for another job if that's your passion, if not, take time to see what you love to do and see if you can create a job around it.

Once you can offer a unique service to humanity, you will always have a job, and you will generate currency which is energy. Some people do not work at all and that is also fine.

"How beautiful is it to rest and do nothing afterwards?"

We must see nature always provides if we surrender, and see we are living in a world of infinite abundance.

We create our reality based on our thoughts and feelings, what you say becomes bond. Changing the words you use to describe your state, will change how you feel about yourself. Saying 'I am worthy' will create a better self image of yourself. Everything is based around perception; the perception we have of ourselves, is far more important than the perception others have of us, that's—the secret.

The passion you have is really your job in disguise.

Chapter Eleven

5 Ways to Build A Better Relationship
"Changing the water of the plant makes it grow"

The greatest relationship we can have is with ourselves. Before we can love anybody, we must begin to love ourselves. The five ways to build a better relationship are: communication, appreciation, passion, trust and fun.

1. Communication.
    The voice is the essence, how we speak to our partner is essential in building a closer bond. Words hold power, it's not the words you use but the energy behind the words. Words mould and shape matter, using words to heal one another, bring the best out of our relationships. Nurturing each other starts with creating free time for one another to express our true feelings.

2. Appreciation.
    Do not take your partner for granted, appreciating your love is a great way to create a harmonious relationship. When we forget to value each other we become complacent, and end up throwing away the very person we cherish. Keeping alive the flame of love requires tremendous dedication and praising your partner every now again will bring you closer together.

3. Passion.
    Deep passion is the driving force of any relationship, the more

passion you two have, the more the relationship thrives. To cultivate passion we must tap into our infinite power by eating healthy organic foods and placing ourselves in an environment which uplifts are spirits. The more energy we can access, the more passion energy is available to us both. As soon as our energy levels decrease our passion begins to wither away like the leaves of a branch.

Letting go of society's expectations and stress, is an awesome way to increase the passion towards each other and live the dream. Allowing your partner to look at someone else and appreciate their beauty frees both of you.

4. Trust.
Trust is essential when building a better relationship. We can only lose what does not belong to us, you cannot force love. Owning someone else is an illusion, you can capture the body, but never the heart—that has to be given to you. Respecting each other to walk in pure freedom is showing how trust can be used, so you both can see a deeper beauty within each other.

5. Have fun.
Building a better relationship is having fun with your partner. Be silly, play games, have a little dance or two. Keeping alive the inner child within each other will bring you both to the first time you set eyes on each other...that magical moment. The magic will begin to blossom, when you can laugh and smile with each other, not taking life so serious. Remember to have fun is to open your heart, both of your hearts will grow with love and you both will be flying in—pure euphoria.

Chapter Twelve

How to Heal Yourself
"The answer lies within."

The only person who can heal yourself is you, no doctor or healer can heal you, they can only act as a guide to help you awaken your infinite power of self healing. Heal yourself by breathing the fresh prana, walk through nature...live in the moment.

The biggest disease you have is not of the body, but of the mind. Once you change the way you think, you can begin to change the way the body heals itself. We live in the world we are thinking of, we create our reality through thoughts and feelings...tangible realities which govern our body universe.

"How does disease begin?"

Many of us our in disease because we are working against the body not with it. Relaxation is what you are, stress is what you think you should be. Stress is the biggest contributor to ill health, and this starts in the mind. Once you change your mind, your whole world changes...the interpretation of what you think is possible.

Scientists say we have over 70 trillion cells within the body, I say we have we have an unlimited amount. Anything is possible, it all starts with belief, it's all B.S: belief systems. We have been told the body is separate from the mind from Newtonian Physics. The body, mind, and spirit are all interconnected—the body is the unconscious mind.

Renee Descartes who is the father of western philosophy brought in the idea of body/mind separation which still reigns supreme. There is no separation in nature, there is only a great relationship based on co-operation. Everything is connected, we exist as one, until we can understand this, we will always be stuck. Disease is an energy imbalance, emanating from our spiritual body, which the mind processes and we feel in our physical bodies. To heal yourself you must love yourself 100%...surrender and accept the body is your loyal servant, working in your favour always.

Letting go of the mind is essential for the body to work to its optimum performance—thought is an interference. Living in the moment, we tap into the field of our true unlimited potential, we open the gift—the present. We must take responsibility and see we are co-creators, the power lies within.

Belief plays a huge role in healing, if you say my disease is incurable you are right, if you say my disease is curable you are right. Opening ourselves to a world of infinite possibilities is essential to allow our body to reach its highest infinite potential.

Embrace nature and learn how everything coexists in harmony with one another. We have three big misperceptions in science regarding the health and wellbeing of ourselves.

The first misperception is we only live in a material universe. Isaac Newton the father of Western Physics thought we lived in a universe of fixed laws and the human being was a well behaved machine.

Ancient cultures have always seen an united universe where everything is connected. They saw a 'spirit' dwelt within each of us, this was the driving force of our creation. In ancient China they saw how the body was comprised of infinite energy fields and called the energy points, 'meridians.' The flow of energy around the body was called 'the mircocosmic orbit.'

By applying pressure to certain areas of the body, this relieved tension and created perfect health. 'Acupuncture' helps unblock the energy flow to create harmony in the body. Quantum physicists now seeing the spirit as an intelligent energy field.

The second misperception is our genes control our biology. Biologists have found a new form of genetics called 'Epigentics.' They say instead of our genes being deterministic, our genes actually have unlimited potential, and our influenced by our environment. Our environment is changing our genes, the genes activate from the outside in.

We exist only in relationship to everything around us. The new paradigm embraces our freedom and sees we are not victims of fate but the power lies inside our hands.

The third misperception of science is an extension of Darwinian belief. Charles Darwin a British Scientist proposed the idea of 'survival of the fittest' in nature—eat or be eaten.

The new paradigm is recognising abundance is our natural state and seeing how evolution is based on cooperation. Competition is an illusion... there is more than enough to go around.

The ideas of separation and competition are the foundation for western thinking—we must come together.

"Why are we the only species on the planet paying for food and accommodation?"

"What a joke!"

The food of the planet should be free and we should use it to heal ourselves. Eating organic foods can raise the vibration and increase a heightened state of wholeness and wellbeing in the body. Raw foods activate our power and pineal gland.

Decalcifying the pineal gland is essential for activating our true power. The ancients have called the pineal gland the seat of intuition, our connection to our primordial life force energy. Allopathic medicine is the medical paradigm the majority live by. This when doctors only treat the symptoms not the underlying causes.

The new way is naturopathic medicine, which treats the root causes of the disease—prevention is better than cure. The symptoms of the body, are the body's way of healing itself. Mucus helps the body eliminate toxins, by taking a cough suppressant you work against the body. The body is your greatest servant, working towards harmonious equilibrium forever.

Opening your heart is essential for self healing, we must live more in our hearts, than our minds.

The heart sends out more electromagnetic signals than any other organ in the body. The heart has its own intrinsic nervous system, therefore we must take care of our heart maintaining inner balance. Many of us live in the left brain of linear thinking, the right brain is connected to the heart.

The new paradigm is where we fuse the left and right brain hemispheres together to become superhuman. In nature we see the metamorphosis of the butterfly from a caterpillar, this process mirrors the evolution of human consciousness.

The caterpillar's later stages show it eating its heart out and everything in sight, it becomes paralysed by its own greed. The cells undergo a process called 'apoptosis' coming from the Greek word meaning falling off, the cells commit suicide.

Lying in the chrysalis the caterpillar turns into ooze as the cells break down. A mystery occurs when out of the blue, 'Imaginal Cells' begin appearing and forming small clusters, they are not of the same DNA as the caterpillar. The caterpillar fights of these 'Imaginal Cells,' however they join forces with other imaginal cells. These 'Imaginal Cells,' although the minority, because of their unity, they become the genetic directors of the caterpillar. They form wings and some them form legs, until we see the miracle of the—butterfly.

There is a parallel between the metamorphosis of the butterfly and the evolution of human consciousness. In the new paradigm we have some groups of people encouraging humanity to tap into their true potential, however, they are met with resistance, even sometimes called 'crazy.'

More people are speaking their minds about planet Earth, and uniting with kindred spirits, these are the—'Imaginal Cells.' Only a few people are needed to change the world and ignite Earth's metamorphosis to a higher state.

The butterfly shows us becoming lighter is the only way to fly. Music is the universal language, sound can prevent and heal you from disease.

High vibration music is key in these times.

We have to not want to be healed from disease, we must see ourselves already healed. When you say, I want, you are sending a signal to the universe you do not have something, therefore it will keep you in lack.

Once you can say I am healed, I am worthy; the universe grants your wishes, after all it's the...infinite genie.

The body is the physical machine, the mind is the software, and the spirit is the power supply—the reservoir of unlimited energy. An analogy is the body is like a water bottle, the mind is the water, and the spirit is the driving force moving the water...we are incredible.

Chapter Thirteen

A New Paradigm
"Time to Fly...Are You Ready?"

Are you ready for the new world? Right here in nature, welcome to the new paradigm. Around the globe many people feel the energy rising within themselves pouring outwards. There is a great shift happening in so many lives, it's not external date, or calendar, it's the metamorphorsis happening within ourselves. Moving from a catepillar into a butterfly, seeing we have to reclaim our power as free sovereign spirits on Earth.

The new paradigm is becoming aware, we do not have to look outside of ourselves, everything exists within us. The search is over. People are becoming their own guru, looking towards each other for a source of support, inspiration and strength.

Each one of us is a master, there are masters all amongst us, but it starts with—knowing thyself.

We are all stars. This a time on the planet where we move from belief into knowing. Ancients have called this the 'age of the water bearer.' We do not have to go on living like this, there is always another way. Breaking the spell of universal mind control, which has left many in a daze, liberates us.

The new paradigm is where we take full responsibility for our internal condition. We have to create our own universe.

"How will you create the new world without money?"

By doing what you love, you receive currency—money is energy... whatever you give out, you will receive back. The universe always sends back what you give to it, it's a gigantic mirror. Many of us in the new paradigm are not focusing all our attention on the media and 'new world order.' The only thing that matters is what's within yourself. The journey within is the most essential—Nobody can do that for you...we must become free once again on the planet.

Religion has kept many in bondage, however, it's part of the 'Earth School training.' The true temple is within, seeing this liberates you. Honouring the animals as sacred is the first step to accessing your higher nature, no life is better than the other. There is no right or wrong way to live, every action is based on resonance.

The new paradigm is one of sharing, where kindred spirits around the whole world will be creating a new infrastructure. The time has come.

Life does not have to be suffering, don't die trying to make it, abundance is our natural state...being free is our birthright.

The two choices for the two paradigm are love or fear? We can go on like this or we can make a change. The change has to come from within.

Create your own value system. When we no longer need value from jobs, when you create your own job...you create your own economy. There is an information overload on the planet, however, true knowing comes from within. Reading all the books in the world will not help you, you must read the greatest of all books...yourself.

Read your body awareness and emotions, and ask yourself:

"How do I feel?"

We must sail beyond knowledge because we are infinite. Tapping into your infinite nature, shows you there is no one way to develop inner clarity. Nature is the greatest book, by looking at one flower you have the equivilant of 50,000 encloypaedias. A picture is worth a thousand words.

Know thyself and see you are worthy to live in bliss...sublime joy. The true gift lies when you see and open it...do not take it for granted. Everyday I give thanks, reverence, and praise—it never had to happen, but it did.

The new paradigm is where we have fun and let go. Some people say life should be taken seriously. The more you tap into your inner child, and have fun...the more creation takes places. We are co-creators, made from the same fabric as the universe. The universe is infinite creations, possibilities, and expressions. There is no beginning or end—we exist outside of time...we transcend it.

The heart space is opening for millions of people in the new paradigm, where we do not live in our minds, instead our hearts. Many of us have become prisoners of our own mind, we've entered a system based on rigid rules and boundaries. Seeing we do not have to go along to get along, you can become unique and different...love yourself 100%.

The heart space opens through self acceptance and appreciation. The heart is the key. What the heart already knows, the brain can only dream of. By many shutting down their hearts, they have become desensistised, the new paradigm is where we express ourselves 100%.

To express yourself you must open your heart, see everything you have learnt is part of a program. Opening up your heart frees you from all programs. We receive the organic download from the cosmos, when the heart expands.

"Should I say this, Maybe I shouldn't say this? Will they like me? Maybe they will not like me?"

All of this is the mind. The mind deals in fear...analytically. The new paradigm is where we fuse the left and right brain hemispheres together. Creative people live in their right brains, and logical people live in their left. The right brain deals with the left side of the body—focusing on knowing. The left deals with the right side of the body—focusing on logic. When you fuse the two together, you become...super powerful. Now the creative side expresses itself, while also you can navigate in the matrix system...smile.

The new paradigm consists of loving yourself—embracing you do not have to be perfect. Ask yourself:

"Do you like the reflection you see in the mirror?"

For eternity, Earth's vibration has been low, now we are rising higher... we are awake. Changing thoughts, changes your feelings and actions... creating a new world—starts with you...time to fly.

Bonus Chapter One

How to Deal With People That Judge You?
"The universe gives everyone a job."

Why do we judge others? Why do they judge us? What's wrong with you? What's wrong with me?

Many look at people and do not like their hair, skin colour, car, personality, boyfriend, girlfriend...what's happening here?

Whenever we judge others, it emanates from our fear, and separation. When you feel separate from everything around you, then you judge it. When you are connected to something, there is no need to judge.

Feeling intimidated by others is another cause for our judgement. To stop worrying, start living, let go...knowing you have no control of what others think or feel. We can only control our response to people's actions.

The best way to deal with people who judge or label you is to be silent. Some people want to debate with us, if we are silent, we do not give them food or energy to feed on. The food we feed other people's energies...give them a greater appetite.

Silence helps others to look at themselves in the mirror, to say:

"What kind of a person am I?"

Many people need a reality check. We are living in a muilti-dimensional universe of infinite life forms, therefore many people are seeing the world in different ways. Everyone is incarnating for different reasons, everyone is on their own evolutionary journey. Accept not everyone will be like you, this is essential—friction is required for things to move around in the...cosmos.

Do not pay attention to petty worries. Someone can only enter your inner kingdom through an invitation. There are many haters out there, but love your haters, as they help reveal your true character.

"Who are you inviting into your house?"

When someone is annoying, do not give them the power of a 'hater,' otherwise you are placing them as an enemy....they have no power.

How we define others determines how much power we give away. Many times we are not other people's issues, we think we are, but going back you find their problems existed before we arrived on the scene. People are dealing with a lot in this 3D reality, a lot of people need someone to take out anger and frustration...do not let it be you. Staying balanced and neutral is essential for maintaining inner equilibrium.

Children live in a state of non judgement, there is no separation... they are free to fly. As we proceed through life we become overwhelmed and disconnected from nature. Many sell souls, and die in the process. On the road to riches, that's what 'The Wizard of Oz' explored...you never checked behind the curtain. Life is a loop, we go around in a circle, and are tested, until we—surrender.

This is 'Earth School,' you end up where you first started, it does not matter what direction you take. Once you have lost your soul you become something else, this is why so many people judge...we are repressed.

Dead food from butchered animals fills the plates of many, ask yourself:

"The people who judge you, where is their heart space?"

Do not take it personal. Some people choose to shut down their hearts and become cold and frosty. The people who judge are stiff and cannot move, when you are fluid, you flow like water—letting go of all judgements.

Maybe you have family members who do not approve of your lifestyle, remember: everyone sees, but not everyone sees the world with the same lens. We only see the world according to our own vibration. As you change your vibration, so does your environment. Many people are stuck at a particular vibration, right here in the underworld, therefore, many reside in their lower nature. These people will always judge because they are separate from their authentic selves...their higher nature. Brush it off and breathe easy when dealing with people who judge you.

The more you pay attention to something, the more it costs, that's why they call it 'paying attention,' because you are at an expense. Liberate yourself from other people's undesirable energies and grudges. Sometimes, people love you, then hate you...then love you again. The problems of others have nothing to do with us—we act as mirrors, mirroring back to each other. Someone sees you and you mirror back something they do not want to see within themselves.

Accept you cannot please everyone. Many of us want the world to love us, we are gladiators in the arena, screaming:

"Are you not entertained?"

Surrender to yourself by letting go...it's time to be free—be happy.

Bonus Chapter Two

How to Stop Absorbing Other People's Energy?

"You turn into what your tuned into."

E veryday I wake up...I say:
     "I am not in this world to live up to your expectations, you do your thing, I do mine, and if by chance we meet that's beautiful, but if not, well that cannot be helped."

There are a number of tools I deal with, to not absorb other people's energy. There are many people around the globe who are very sensitive, some people call them 'psychics.'

Everybody is a psychic, we just have various degrees of sensitivity. Highly sensitive people have the ability to mind read, even when they are not speaking. Entering a room they can attract tremendous energy, they feel what everybody is feeling inside the room. Feeling can be a great gift, especially in a desensitised world; but how do we protect ourselves from other people's energy?

There is a term called the 'Intuitive Empath.' Empathy is different from sympathy; empathy is the ability to recognise other people's emotions; sympathy is feeling compassion for other people. Empathy is 'feeling into' other people, you place your mind inside theirs and you embody what they are going through.

There are five ways which have helped me on my journey to stop absorbing other people's energy and toxic junk:

1 .   Remember...you cannot please everyone.

Accept not everyone is going to like you, once you can get past that, you do not absorb other people's energy. Everyone on this planet is here for a different reason, living their own universal life journey. Some people love you, some hate you; but there are no positive or negative people—only resonance.

"Please love me, please me my friend."

There are many people in the world who are too nice, they always say:

"Why do nice people finish last."

There is nothing wrong with being nice, it is more important however to be yourself. Once you stay true to yourself, you do not absorb other people's energy...because you are loving and accepting yourself 100%. If people do not like you for who you are, too bad, they can hit the road...I'm sorry.

2 .   The invitation.

Choose whether or not, you would like to be invited to where this person is going to take you. Nobody can enter our dominion, which is our inner kingdom, a universe within itself—without an invitation.

We attract every single person into our lives. We have to see, many of us leave food...food is the invitation for people to come inside the house, the temple within you.

When there is no food at someone's house, nobody goes, however if your neighbour has a scrumptious banquet...everybody flocks there. We have to remember we are consciously or unconsciously inviting people. Not absorbing other people's energy is to remind ourselves the power lies within, to choose whether we want to invite this person into our temple... which is within ourselves.

3. Do not pay attention.

A lot of people are called 'energy vampires.' An energy vampire is someone who uses your energy to survive, in essence a parasite. A parasite can only live on the host body. They call it paying attention for a reason, because everything in the universe is a process of exchange...the universe is a great business man/woman.

The law of exchange is the law of nature. When you pay someone attention, you are giving them energy. We have to change our focus to stop absorbing other people's energy. Whatever you focus on grows.

Energy vampires work by making you think of them, thoughts are energy, therefore they steal your thoughts—energy is currency...currency is money.

Feelings of exhaustion follow after encountering energy vampires.

We have to remember where we pay attention.

"Are we focusing on what we want, or are we focusing on what we fear?"

Let go, know your worth, do not allow anybody else to give you value, that's how to stop absorbing other people's energy—we must let go off society's expectations.

4. Breathe.

Going into nature can purify your senses, the fresh 'chi' circulating allows a greater freedom within the body, you feel light, fun and free.

Meditating helps to not absorb other people's energy, meditation is not only sitting in a lotus pose, it may be dancing, singing...your unique expression of inner freedom.

Purify the water within yourself, change the water, become fluid like the water...become like the butterfly.

"Have you ever noticed why you cannot catch a butterfly?"

A butterfly is sensitive, but does not absorb your energy...it is wise. The butterfly moves in a light manner, moving at fast high speeds, therefore the trick of the secret...while you are breathing, you are increasing your vibration. The more you slow down, the more you absorb other people's energy.

Breathing increases the blood flow circulation around the body, you feel calmer, thus you do not absorb other people's energy.

Keep your head up—the secret's of body language.

How we carry ourselves in the world, says so much about how we see ourselves. Remember, once you look down, you are inviting people to steal your energy. Walk with confidence, with self esteem, know that you are worthy...you are deserving. Do not let anybody make you feel inferior, because in essence, there is nobody greater than yourself.

When the caterpillar is there, consuming all of the food, becoming greedy, it is absorbing energy, therefore it cannot move. Becoming lighter is the only way to fly and stop absorbing other people's energy.

Keep it moving just like a butterfly, become an alchemist, become a transformer. We have to change our internal condition before we can change our external condition—that's the secret.

5. Take responsibility for your internal condition.

How you feel inside is how you project yourself externally. The body is the unconscious mind, become aware of your body, ask yourself:

"How do I feel?"

By taking 100% responsibility of feelings, you see other people's problems are not yours, this frees you from absorbing other people's energy. We live in a world of infinite possibilities, infinite creations, infinite expressions, therefore, the universe gives everybody a job.

Nature has a sense of humour, nature is sending people into our lives to test us...your greatest adversary is your greatest friend.

The people who are draining our energy, do not give them power, what you fight you give energy to. Tap into your authenticity 100%, take responsibility...you are a co-creator.

We are creating our own reality based on thoughts and feelings. Everything is based around perception, the perception we have of ourselves, is greater than the perception others have of us...that's the secret. Become aware, once you change your perception, you change your reality—that's how to stop absorbing other people's energy.

Perception coming from the Latin 'percipio' meaning 'the apprehension with senses.' Everything is based on how we see ourselves, that is the secret of perception, it all lies within us...the image we have of ourselves.

"How do you see yourself?"

"Am I a victim?"

Once you see yourself as a victim, you give other people power over you—therefore you start absorbing their energy. Nobody has power unless you give them power.

Changing what others think of you is an illusion—fly...let go of fear today. Fear is false evidence appearing real. Many of us are stuck in fear, to move past fear we have to embrace ourselves for who we are. It's not about fitting in on the planet:

"Please like me, please be my friend."

Through indoctrination, subliminal programming, mind control, many from childhood are told they have to fit in. We have to be the same, dress the same, act the same, laugh at the same things. All we have to do is be ourselves 100%...love yourself.

The more you connect with yourself, the more empathy you can show to others. Embracing nature activates your pineal gland, which is the seat of your intuition...so now you pick up everyone's feelings and emotions—you project yourself into other people's personalities.

This may be liberating, but if you do not know how to stop absorbing other people's energy...it will become a problem.

Many people in society are 'cognitive misers.' This is where people choose not to worry about anybody else.

Through the fluoride in water, bad food diets, and attitudes, many people's pineal glands have become calcified. By choosing not to become aware we are living in a world of infinite possibilities...it calcifies the pineal gland. Psychopaths do not show empathy because they are desensitised.

To stop absorbing other people's energy, we must remember, we attract what we are. We have to place ourselves in environments which boost our spirits—thus raising our vibration and frequency. Like attracts like.

Absorbing someone's energy is not positive or negative, we give people permission. Everything in nature is based on a symbiotic relationship. There is a relationship between the sun and the ocean, between the moon and the plants. Everything is based on sharing in nature. To stop absorbing other people's energy, ask yourself:

"Does this person make me feel good? And am I making them feel good?"

"Is there an equal exchange of energy here?"

"Or is it lopsided on the scales? One person is taking all my energy."

We have a choice of where we want to be, of where we place ourselves in this universe...the power lies within you.

Remembering you are worthy to have to most limitless, expansive, marvellous existence...frees you.

"Why do we spend our whole day, ruminating on someone who is insignificant?"

Brushing it off, letting go, and moving past petty thoughts—help us not to absorb other people's energy.

The secret to stop absorbing other people's energy is to change what you tune into. Many of us watch hours of television, which tells lies to your vision. We have to tell our own vision...tell-our-vision.

Programs such as talk shows, may be beneficial to grasp human nature, but many of us absorb harmful energy, thus we are drained after watching. The programs serve as distractions, to keep us like programmed robots, zombies...drones—wake up.

The human brain is a giant antennae, a transmitter and receiver of information, therefore we have to become conscious of what channel we are tuning into.

By changing your channel, you change your focus and do not absorb other people's energy. Like the television, if you do not want to watch a program, you change the channel, so you do not have to absorb that energy. The secrets of nature reveal themselves in all aspects of our lives, if only we would open our eyes to see.

Women connect to the universe through their womb, which is the star gate. The gateway between two worlds, spirit and matter. Many women feel through their wombs...it talks to them, it is their seat of intuition. Women have to protect their wombs to stop absorbing other people's energy and junk.

Cultivate the womb, place it in healing energies, go to nature, take a walk...talk a swim...jump up and down—feel alive.

We have to feel alive to stop absorbing other people's energy, live, breathe —enjoy life.

Many nice people feel if I am polite, that's all I need to get through life. "No!"

We have to be direct and true to ourselves.

"Say what you mean, and mean what you say."

Be yourself...the power of 'No.'

This will take you far in life, say it with confidence, set energetic boundaries. Once you can say 'no' to people with confidence, you stop absorbing everyone's undesirable energy.

Many so called 'nice people' deny themselves the truth, because they want to make everyone feel happy, they are afraid of saying 'no' to anyone. They do not want to hurt other people's feelings and upset them. In essence, they upset themselves by refusing to listen to their inner oracle which is their—heart.

Sound is an amazing way to stop absorbing other people's energy, everything is based on vibration in the universe. Music is the universal language. Once you can heal yourself through sound, listening to music which uplifts your spirit, it helps us to become neutral.

Natural ocean salt water can help us stay neutral, by changing the cells, helping our DNA structure to be more in harmony with our body.

Intuition comes from the Latin 'intueri' meaning to 'look at' or to 'gaze upon.' The more we connect with ourselves, the more we notice the intricate designs of nature.

Such a gift it is to have a deep intuition, however, we have to remember how to protect ourselves from harmful energy.

Have fun, smile, you cannot catch a butterfly, although the butterfly is sensitive, it has mastered the secrets of the universe...it is flying, so light, so free—so powerful.

We have to become that butterfly, sensitive, but at the same time projecting ourselves from harmful energies...the power lies within yourself.

Bonus Chapter Three

How To Overcome Any Fear
"Fear is the greatest energy vampire."

Fear is necessary in fight of flight moments, but many of us fear events which have not happened.

"How do we free ourselves from fear?"

Fear is a self created feeling, emanating from an imagery belief, based on the illusion of separation. To let go of fear we have to start loving and accepting ourselves 100%. Embracing nature, breathing in the fresh air, eating foods which increase our vibration, all of this helps alleviate fear.

The power lies within, ultimately we have to let go 'of' society's expectations.

"What do you fear?"

The greatest fear may be death. Some people fears include: flying, looking people in the eyes, public speaking, commitment in a relation-ships, changing their diets, aliens, the new world order, spiders, body image, failure, rejection, and accepting and loving yourself 100%.

"How do we become fearless and let go off society's expectations?"

The fear is never in the moment, it is in the past or future, the power is in the now. To let go of fear, we have to tap into the present moment.

There are many things around, to make us afraid of this vast world, but fear is the greatest energy vampire...the more we are in fear, the more we lose our energy. Throughout my journey, I have found five great ways to overcome any fear:

1 . Face your fear.

Look your fear straight in the eyes, feel the fear and do it anyway; embrace the challenge the universe is sending you. Go for it...fear is always making us rise higher.

Fear never takes place. Fear is the waiting for something to happen—the anticipation of what never comes. When something happens we fear:

"Then what?"

We look for another fear...ask yourself:

"What is the worst thing that could happen?"

"When it does happen, how does it make me feel?"

Seeing we can overcome one fear enables us the strength to overcome=another fear.

2 : Do not externalise your power.

Many of us on the planet have given away our power to someone or something, we feel is more superior than ourselves. Maybe through a religion, guru, political party, feeling someone has cursed us—therefore we externalise power...now we are victims. Whenever you see yourself as a victim, you will always remain in fear.

Taking back your power is key to overcome fear. When we see we are the architects our own reality, it lets the fear out. We create our own reality through every single thought we have.

Everything we see is based on our perception, how you see world.

"You turn into what your tuned into."

By not feeling worthy, we lose power, giving someone else power over our lives, thus making us more fearful. We must never let anyone place value over our lives, we must give ourselves our unique=value system.

Not externalising power means taking 100% responsibility for our thoughts and feelings...our entire internal condition. We create our experiences in life, other people come, but it is us who chooses how we respond to situations and people within our lives. We have to reclaim our power—start smiling

3. Do not justify your fear
In your childhood, your brother/sister may have put a spider on you, while you were sleeping...now you fear spiders forever. By rationalising your fear, you remain a prisoner of your fear, because you are allowing yourself a reason to hold onto the fear.

We tell ourselves this fear is coming from the outside, rather than the inside. The power lies within us, by no longer making an excuse for the fear, we can move past the fear...there is no reason for its existence. The fear is not serving a purpose, it is not creating a well being within our—body.

4. Change your belief
It's all B.S.—belief systems. Changing your mind, changes your world, it changes the relationship you have to fear, therefore liberating you of it. Belief is powerful, if you say i can overcome this fear, you are right, if you say i cannot overcome this fear...you are right.

Many of our fears emanate from not feeling we are good enough or worthy...all of that has to—disappear.

5. Let go of judgment
The more you judge, the more you separate, separation is the foundation of fear. Separation is your only disease, it is the cause everything else is the effect. Everything is connected, I am another yourself... now.

So long as we have fear in our hearts we cannot be free

We have to see where we are directing our energy too, many of us on the planet are addicted to fear, ask yourself:

"Are you focusing on what you want, or what you fear?"

Fear has become the medicine of the masses. Reading newspapers and watching the television increases our fear, thus widening our appetite for more fear. We become what we tune into...the only thing to fear is fear itself. Ask yourself:

"This feeling I am creating (because I am a co-creator) how is it serving me?"

"Is it empowering me or is it taking away my energy?"

Fear energy is only powerful when it stays inside, when it comes out it has no power, let the fear go, do not give yourself a reason to hold on.

Become aware of body awareness...the body is the unconscious mind.

The body is always communicating to us. The body, mind , spirit, are all interconnected. Aligning your body, aligns your mind and thus aligns your spirit in perfect harmony.

A tense body means you have a tense mind, showing you have a tense spirit; the three are interchangeable. There is a pattern throughout everything in existence. Finding time to reconnect back to your body is essential to—overcome fear.

To overcome fear, we have to release tension within the body. Fear is muscle memory, stored within the body; fear now becomes a pattern within the body. Many people afraid of direct eye contact put their heads down towards the ground.

This creates muscular tension within the neck, leaving fear imprints, now fear becomes a part of the body...a muscle memory. When you change the relationship with your body through healing practices, your heal your mind, because you are reprogramming the fear=making it vanish.

Energy is stored within our minds...that is the secret. Fear and love are stored within the body. Many people are afraid to smile...to smile to be free from fear...you are expanding.

The more you frown, the more your muscles contract, making you more fearful. The body never lies, now the fear has left an energetic signature on the body.

"How are we carrying ourselves?"

How we carry ourselves externally is how we feel internally. The power lies within you, in every single action, we are creating our own reality.

Some people say:

"We are governed by everything around us."

To an extent, it is true. We do not have control of what happens to us, but we do have control over how we respond. In relation to fear, we must change are reaction to a situation, before with change our interaction to that situation.

Attitude is also a great way to overcome fear.

"How do you see things?"

The same event happened to two people, but they never saw it in the same way. Each one is taking a different attitude, therefore each one is dealing with fear in a different way.

Attitude creates a blood chemistry within the body. Fear is a chemical, once you take back your power, you see as your attitude changes, so does the types of chemicals being released from the brain...phenomenal.

Many of us our fears emanate from our lifestyles...from the foods we eat. Foods like mangos, dates, kale, spinach, and oranges have healing vibrations. Every food carries a particular vibration.

Food can be used to heal us from fear. Many fearful people tend to have a refined diet of pure junk food. On my journey, I found moving towards a planet based diet, eating more sun foods—fear disappeared.

"You are what you eat, drink and think."

Everything is intertwined, we must look at all areas of life whilst dealing with fear.

"Does the music I listen to, leave me with a sense of calm, or maximise my fear?"

"Are we connecting to kindred spirits, or focusing on people who steal our energy?"

All of these questions must be asked to overcome fear.

Fear of the unknown is common among many, we fear the uncertainty of life, this is the 'existential anxiety.' Some people are afraid of death... upon seeing we are living in a transient universe.

There is nothing to worry over, energy cannot be destroyed, only transferred, you body may die...but your spirit will live on forever. Tapping into our inner child helps us embrace the unknown—remember when everything was mysterious.

"Have you ever wondered why children do not fear like adults?"

Children are powerful, because they are tuned into the present moment...a place where fear does not live. Life is continuous process, the past, present, and future are all happening simultaneously.

Children are connected to the source. The more you live out of the present moment, the more you deviant from source, which is a part of yourself. We are made from the same fabric as the universe...the universe does not want you to be afraid.

"Is that why you were created?"

"Was I put on planet Earth to be and live in perpetual fear 24/7?"

When we turn of the TV, we see wars and a scary world, letting go of fear restores inner balance in your kingdom...within yourself.

To overcome fear we have to tune and keep alive the inner child within us.

Balanced body, balanced, mind, balanced spirit...the original trinity.

Overcoming fear is about looking at the words we use. Words are powerful vibrations, the word grammar, coming from the Old English word 'grimoire' meaning 'book of spells.'

Everything we speak is a spell of some sort, words were created to hide the truth. By changing the words you use, this helps overcome certain fears.

"I can't...No...I can."

By saying 'I can,' this re-programmes your whole body; it remoulds every single cell within your body.

Once you say 'I can,' your cells are working for you, once you say, 'I can't,' your cells are working against you. Saying 'I can't,' closes you off to a world of infinite possibilities...everything is possible...nothing is impossible.

Words can be used as positive affirmations to heal yourself and over= come fear. Use words to inspire and uplift your spirits, we are talking to our cells...even when we are not speaking.

Talking to your heart, liver and pancreas can remove fearful energies from these powerful organs.

"What energy am I directing to these organs?"

"Is it an energy of fear, or is it an energy of love?"

There are only two energies in the universe, ask yourself:

"What are we inviting into are sacred space within ourselves...fear or love?"

The power lies within our hands, we have to be ready to use it when we're ready.

Having a light heart is the best way to overcome fear...have fun. Many of us hold onto fearful baggage by justifying it; we say I need to hold onto the fear, because the moment we let go...then we let go of the experiences of what's happened to us.

"No!"

We can forgive...we do not have to forget; we can let go of the fearful energies, which are only harming ourselves to a greater degree.

So many people on the planet live in fear, fear breeds a whole host of other negative emotions such as: guilt, hate, anxiety, stress, panic and anger.

All of this builds to a crescendo, until we become stuck.

We turn into the very things we are afraid of.

In my early journey, I was afraid of the 'powers that be,' then I realised we are the powers that be; because we are creating our 'own' reality. We are the power plant creating every single experience in our reality...it's all coming from our perception.

"You are powering your reality, you are the glue holding everything in place"

We have a phenomenal power, once we connect together with like minds, supporting each other...together we can help each other overcome fear=united we thrive.

We need to know what is happening around the globe, yes, but ask yourself:

"Is it liberating you? Or is it making you a prisoner of your own mind?"

"To do, or to be?"

That is the question. Many people on the planet are caught in doing, we always have to be somewhere...this takes ourselves away from the present moment, therefore making us more prone to fear.

By letting go, moving from doing into being...you overcome fear=you allow yourself to surrender to the present moment. All we have to do is become ourselves authentically—and love it.

The more people think for themselves, the more they let go of fear, because their fears are not theirs; it is the media's and their society...it has been implanted in your mind from childhood.

This is what is keeping you in bondage and in slavery—it frees you to see this. The fears we have are not our own. Many people fight in wars on behalf of their country, some people do not like certain people because they are raised in cultures and traditions which tell them not to.

We have to be free from all man-made dogma and law. There is only universal law, we have to align ourselves to that...the only authority is nature.

We have to let go of any kind of separation—all of this is the root of our fears and our concerns.

To overcome fear we have to 'Know Thyself.' So many of us spend our entire life going out of ourselves, we have to travel the journey within ourselves to discover who we are.

"I am not a democrat, republican, conservative, a lawyer, my job, my skin colour, religion, nationality, or race...I am none of these things."

When I saw this on my journey, it freed me from fear.

To overcome fear we must let go of all labels—let go off society's expectations.

Let go of other people's definition...create your own.

Dance, be free and at one with nature...learn from everything around you.

Remember we came here to—live free...have fun.

A Note From The Author

Ralph Smart is an Author, Psychologist, Alchemist, Researcher, Radio Host, Musician, Graphic Designer, Film Maker, & Infinite Being. Ralph Smart was born in London. He has travelled to five continents. He enjoys nature, and meeting people from all spectrums of life. Awarded with a 'BA Combined Honours' in: 'Psychology' and 'Criminology'-human nature fascinates him.

The founder of 'Infinite Waters,' a media channel on 'Youtube' showcasing gripping documentaries and videos, regarding unlocking true human potential and being a limitless being.

Ralph has also just published his debut novel: Tryathon: the love of a galaxy—A novel taking a glimpse into the potential future, the digital age, where wars are fought through technology.

Above all Ralph knows all humans were born to be free—Being free is our birthright.

Infinite Waters Website: http://infinitewaters.net/

Tryathon Website: http://infinitewaters.net/books

Email: infinitewaters@gmail.com

Youtube Channel: www.youtube.com/kemetprince1

Stay Diving Into Infinite Waters :)

CPSIA information can be obtained
at www.ICGtesting.com
Printed in the USA
LVHW110746030621
689197LV00006B/1012

9 780956 897367